THE MBA GUIDE TO NETWORKING LIKE A

Rockstar

*The Ultimate Guide to Navigating the Complex MBA
Landscape & Developing Personal Relationships to
Stand Out Among Top-Caliber Candidates*

Cover design and graphics by Brian A. Miller | Author photograph by Heather P. Miller

Printed in the United States of America   *First printing 2011*

ISBN 978-0-615-48705-2

For

my constant sources of support & inspiration.

My family, especially:
My wonderful parents: Mina & Jitendra
My beautiful sisters (and awesome brother-in-law): Rina & Sejal (and Mital)
My adorable nephews and nieces: Anand, Amit, Dia & Aditi
My always-loving and super-amazing grandmas: Lalitaba and Lilaba

My friends and mentors, especially:
My eighth-grade English teacher: William Semins
My college advisor who showed me what leadership is: Dr. William J. Blake
My "first boss": Russ Kitsemble

For people I've met along the way, who inspire me to always continue
exploring the world and continue learning about myself

For aspiring MBAs who want to change the world—don't lose your vision

Contents

Introduction: The Underdog/i

1   Science of Networking/1

2   The MBA Networking Lifecycle/9

3   The Corporate Presentation/19

4   The Post-Corporate Presentation Networking Reception/27

5   One-on-One Conversations/39

6   Closed-List Events & Interview Invitations/49

7   Off-Campus Networking & Events/57

8   Securing the Internship or Full-Time Offer/67

9   Self Assessment & Determining Fit/75

10   Tools & Real Examples/89

11   Being You! How to Stay Genuine While Networking Like a Rockstar/125

Epilogue: Networking for a Lifetime/129

A Note to Part Time Students: You Gotta Work Harder!/135

Key Terms and Definitions/141

SPECIAL ACKNOWLEDGEMENT

I especially want to thank Valerie Banner, who helped me write this book. I greatly value her expertise as an experienced writer who has been published nationally in magazines, newspapers and online. With a keen writing and editing eye, she helped me convey the many ideas and concepts that I wanted to capture in this book. Her skills, knowledge and continuous support helped make this book possible.

i

Yes. No. Maybe. Rockstar. It's the same every time. After you've lived it, you see the pattern. When a recruiter "meets" you (in person, on the phone, through your resume, etc.), he or she immediately places you into one of four categories: Yes, no, maybe or Rockstar.

This decision directly impacts whether you get to interview for that dream job—or not. What most of us don't realize is that you can influence the recruiter's decision mindset to land in—or even move into—the Rockstar category. The only problem is: It's not easy to figure out.

In my two years at B-school, I figured it out and I made the system work for me—and that's what I want to share with you in this guide. Many believe their resume is their ticket to career success. Recruiters use resumes for a reason: They provide a way to look at hundreds of candidates in a similar format. However, they also reduce an entire person to an 8.5″ x 11″ piece of paper.

When looking at me on a piece of paper, not many firms would have jumped at the chance to interview me. I was a *maybe* at best. By reading my resume, a recruiter only would learn that I had an average GMAT score, had attended a lesser known undergraduate university and had little more than two years of work experience.

So how did I manage to interview with every top firm that I was interested in?

Networking.

> *I used networking to break free of the constraints of an 8.5″ x 11″ piece of paper.*

> *I used networking to personally connect with the firms in which I was interested.*

> *I used networking to show recruiters that I was a Rockstar.*

After a while, it became more and more like a science to me. Everything that I've learned and leveraged for success is in this guide. And it can work for you too, no matter who you are:

The Superstar

You've got everything going for you. You're smart, look great on paper and can hold a conversation with just about anyone. Still, the MBA networking landscape may be unfamiliar to you and you may lack the right tools to navigate it successfully. This book will reveal the MBA networking lifecycle, teach you how to navigate the "half-moon effect" and provide you with additional tools to be a Rockstar.

The Paper Idol

You've got a resume that shines, but you may be shy or uncomfortable speaking with people in unfamiliar settings or large groups. Essentially, you need to gain confidence in your communication skills. This profile suits many engineers who aren't used to the selling game. International students also may fall into this bucket because they are unfamiliar with U.S. culture and customs. This book contains models for communication and real-life detailed examples to bolster your confidence, in addition to the roadmap of the MBA networking lifecycle. Jump off that 8.5" x 11" piece of paper and take your networking to a whole new level.

The Great Communicator

You can talk the talk, but you might not have that perfect background to show you walked the walk. You may have been an artist or a librarian, or you might not have much work experience. While meeting new people may be easy for you, getting the interview with your dream firm(s) requires more than just people knowing you. They need to know what you bring to the table. This book will help you assess your relative competitiveness and appropriately take actions throughout the MBA networking lifecycle to improve your chances for success—no matter what your background.

While most B-school students will fall into one of these buckets, some may straddle more than one category or be the "surprise" candidate of the class. In addition, part-time students can benefit by understanding the ins and outs of the full-time experience to better prepare for their own unique journey to find career success. This guide is designed to be relevant to all audiences. The content is packed-in, the flow is conversational and organized so you can get the answers to the questions that are most important for you. Maybe you're wondering:

How do I get started?

This guide is designed for the busy MBA student and you can jump ahead to a specific question, but to get the most out of the book, read it from front to back. Networking is a nebulous concept to many, and this guide introduces it within a specific structure, breaking it down into a "science." Each chapter contains topical questions that allow you to jump in where it is most important for you. It is organized into 11 main chapters:

- Chapter 1 – Principles of Networking
- Chapter 2 – The Networking Lifecycle
- Chapter 3 – The Corporate Presentation
- Chapter 4 – The Post-Corporate Presentation Networking Reception
- Chapter 5 – One-on-One Conversations
- Chapter 6 – Closed List Events & Interview Invitations
- Chapter 7 – Off-Campus Networking & Events
- Chapter 8 – Securing the Internship or Full-Time Offer
- Chapter 9 – Self Assessment & Determining Fit
- Chapter 10 – Tools & Real Examples
- Chapter 11 – Being You! How to Stay Genuine While Networking Like a Rockstar

If you're limited on time, jump to the parts that impact you most. Here are the questions answered in each chapter:

Chapter 1: The Science of Networking/1

What is networking, really?/1

Who do I network with and why?/2

How do recruiters think and make decisions?/3

What is the relationship hierarchy, and how
do I leverage it for success?/4

How do I know if I have the *support* of recruiters
or influential individuals?/7

What's my goal when it comes to networking?/7

Chapter 2: The MBA Networking Lifecycle/9

What is the MBA networking lifecycle, and what
is it comprised of?/9

I just got to campus/started my MBA
adventure—what do I need to know?/11

What is the difference between firm-specific and school-specific
influential individuals? How do I interact with each group?/12

How do I know which firms I should pursue?
Is there a way to gauge fit?/15

When is it appropriate to reach out to my dream
firm(s) to maximize my chances of success?/16

There's a company that I'm really interested in. How
important is it that I network with other companies?/17

Chapter 3: The Corporate Presentation/19

What is the on-campus corporate presentation,
and why is it so important?/20

My dream company is having a corporate presentation
event, what should I do to prepare?/20

I'm going to an event tomorrow—what should I bring?/21

During the event, what should I do? How do I get noticed?/22

How should I dress for the corporate presentation?/22

What kinds of questions should I ask during the
corporate presentation?/23

Chapter 4: The Post-Corporate Presentation Networking Reception/27

What is the post-corporate presentation
networking reception, and why is it so important?/27

Who should I network with at the post-corporate
presentation networking reception?/28

What kinds of questions should I ask during the post-corporate
presentation networking reception?/29

What if I ask a stupid question?/30

How do I navigate the half-moon effect at a networking event?/31

Post-Event Protocol/34

Do I need to do anything after the event is over?/34

When should I send the follow-up email/note?/35

What are best practices when it comes to
thank you emails/notes?/35

OK, so I sent my thank-you emails/notes, what do I do
next to get that interview?/36

Chapter 5: One-on-One Conversations/39

One-on-One Conversations: In Person/39
Office Hours/Coffee Chats: These are just relaxed
    conversations, right?/39
What is the recruiter trying to ascertain in
    the conversation? How should I approach it?/41
What if the chat goes horribly wrong?/41
One-on-One Conversations: By Phone/42
I got a positive response to my request for
    a follow-up phone call! What do I talk about?/42
How long should the call be?/43
What are some best practices for the call?/43
How do I end the call?/45
Is it OK to discuss off-topic items?/45
What should I do after the call?/46
What if I've already waited too long to follow up after the call?/46
What if I didn't get a positive response to my request
    for a follow-up phone call?/47

Chapter 6: Closed-List Events & Interview Invitations/49

Closed-List Events/49
I got invited to a closed-list event! What do I do?
    How do I prepare?/49
I didn't get invited to a closed-list event. What do I do?/50
What's my goal when attending a closed-list event?/51
What are the next steps once the event is over?/52
I got an interview! What do I do?/53
I didn't get an interview. What do I do?/54

Chapter 7: Off-Campus Networking & Events/57

What if my dream firm does not recruit on campus?/57
How do I leverage my alumni network or "cold-call"
     potential contacts at my dream firm?/58
What are national networking events, and how can
     they help me get my dream job?/60
I'm going to attend a networking event—what do
     I need to know?/61

Chapter 8: Securing the Internship or Full-Time Offer/67

I got an internship offer! What do I do?/67
I didn't get an internship offer. What do I do?/68
I have been wait-listed, what do I do?/69
I am a student trying to secure a full-time offer
     with a firm I'm interested in but wasn't successful
     with previously. What do I do and when?/70

Chapter 9: Self Assessment & Determining Fit/75

What attributes are recruiters really looking for in a
     Rockstar candidate?/75
How do these attributes vary by firm? How do I ensure
     I properly project my fit with the relevant attributes?/77
How can I assess how strong/weak I am across this
     list of attributes?/78
What can I do to positively impact my networking
     goals if I find one of these attributes to be my strength?/82
What can I do to positively impact my networking goals
     if I find one of these attributes to be a weakness?/84

Chapter 10: Tools & Real Examples/89

How do I start a conversation with a complete stranger?/90
How do I reach out to individuals who are
    not in my personal network (cold-calling)?/93
How personal should I get while networking?/98
What should a thank-you email/note look like?/100
How should a one-on-one phone conversation flow?/108
What should my communications look like if
    I am invited to an event, interview, etc.?/110
What should my communications look like if I am not
    invited to an event, interview, etc.?/110
I am a student trying to secure a full-time offer with a
    firm I'm interested in but wasn't successful with previously.
    What should my communications look like?/116

Chapter 11: Being You! How to Stay Genuine While Networking Like a Rockstar/125

Epilogue: Networking for a Lifetime/129

A Note to Part-Time Students: You Gotta Work Harder!/135

Everything that I learned about the power of effective networking is in this guide—it's now up to you to decide how to best leverage these learnings to help accomplish your career goals. Good luck!

Best,

—*JJP*

1

MBA networking is an adventure: It is dynamic, unusual and often difficult to navigate. Networking in business school varies across campuses, firms and students, so this book is designed to help you understand it better by breaking it down to a "science."

What is networking, really?

Networking is building relationships with influential individuals to positively impact career development. Effective networking is more than just getting exposure, it involves learning who the right people are and building *personal* relationships with them.

Who do I network with and why?

Throughout the MBA networking lifecycle, you will network with a variety of people who either directly or indirectly influence your chances of success.

A *recruiter* is a person, or a member of a group of people, who is directly responsible to make decisions about who is selected for closed-list events and interviews. Usually, the recruiter(s) will be introduced to you so it's easy to know who they are. Larger companies typically have recruiting teams, often comprised of recruiting managers (human resource representatives), school managers (recent alumni/junior firm staff) and/or school sponsors (senior firm staff). Your goal is to understand who the recruiters are and to focus directly on building strong personal relationships with them.

In addition, you will want to build relationships with *influential individuals*, who can *indirectly* influence the Recruiter's Decision Mindset (RDM). This group includes non-recruiting staff from your dream firm(s), members of the alumni association, classmates and even professors or school staff.

The *Recruiter's Decision Mindset (RDM)* is a recruiter's conclusion regarding your candidacy with the firm based on a set of facts, assumptions and interactions throughout the networking lifecycle.

How do recruiters think and make decisions?

As mentioned earlier, a recruiter will make an immediate decision about your fit with their company: yes, no, maybe or Rockstar. Every interaction you have with an influential individual or recruiter impacts this decision. Over time, the RDM can change, and your goal is to ensure a positive trajectory by leveraging all tools and paths available to you.

Effective networking is more than just getting exposure, it involves learning who the right people are, when to interact with them and how to interact with them to positively impact the RDM. While focusing your networking energy on the recruiters is important, you also should connect with influential individuals for a variety of reasons. Some things to keep in mind:

- Some firms make extremely collaborative decisions. If *everyone* on that team isn't on board with a particular candidate, then they may not extend an invitation. In this scenario, if only a few people at that firm know you, then you may get passed over for other candidates who have done a better job of building relationships with multiple influential individuals.

- The recruiter's time is limited and he or she may not be able to give you the time and attention you need—which means you may not have an opportunity to directly impact the RDM. In this scenario, influential individuals can provide feedback on your behalf to positively impact the RDM.

- You may or may not hit it off with the recruiter(s) for a variety of reasons. However, if an influential individual is clamoring for you, then you still may get the interview.

Consequently, to ensure a positive trajectory in advancing the RDM, it is imperative to get to know the right mix of people during the networking lifecycle and enhance your rapport by advancing through the relationship hierarchy.

What is the relationship hierarchy, and how do I leverage it for success?

The relationship hierarchy indicates the level of personal connection between two parties—in this case, the relationship between a candidate and a recruiter/influential individual. Pictured in figure 1, the relationship hierarchy is comprised of four levels: *awareness, consideration, acknowledgement* and *support.*

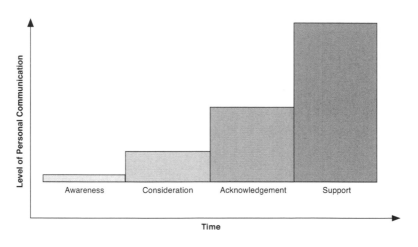

Figure 1: The Relationship Hierarchy

Advancing through the relationship hierarchy with recruiters/influential individuals is an avenue to positively impact the RDM. When you build stronger, closer relationships, you more likely will advance the RDM from no to maybe to yes to Rockstar:

Awareness

The right mix of individuals are *aware* of you. They may have met you, talked to you on the phone or read your resume. You want to advance quickly from *awareness* into the next stage. Otherwise, you risk a recruiter/influential individual making conclusions, which may or may not be accurate, based on only a few facts and interactions. In this stage, you typically have little to no relationship with the recruiter/influential individual.

Consideration

At this stage, the recruiter/influential individual is not only *aware* of you but also *considers* you when discussing recruitment. You are more than just a face or a name; he or she now has some understanding of your capabilities or interests. At this stage, the individual

To help illustrate the relationship hierarchy, let's compare it to a local mayoral race.

Awareness

If you are aware of a candidate running for mayor, but do not know anything else, you will make assumptions about the candidate's capabilities.

Consideration

This is the point when you have met and understand the candidate's background and platform.

Acknowledgement

This is when you tell your neighbor that he should learn more about a candidate because you find her interesting and believe she has a compelling platform.

Support

This is when you might canvass the neighborhood to share your support and excitement for the candidate. It also means you feel you know her well and will vote for her, doing your best to make sure she succeeds in the race.

may know that you are Jenny from New York interested in financial services, and you begin to build a *professional* relationship.

Acknowledgement

Acknowledgement is a strong step forward, occurring when a recruiter/influential individual *acknowledges* you during communication as someone he or she is familiar with and also as someone he or she believes is a potential candidate for the firm. Stemming from positive interactions with you (through email, by phone or in person), this person may know your background, where you come from, some examples of your experience and can tie it all together. This step also includes *acknowledgement* of your requests and interests in the firm. A clear sign of *acknowledgment* is when this person introduces you or refers you to another colleague. Your professional relationship may become more casual and comfortable at this step.

Support

Support is the final step and the most difficult to achieve. While some candidates (e.g., superstars) may advance to the *acknowledgement* step pretty quickly, achieving *support* is still a challenge. Once you advance to this final step, a recruiter/influential individual will treat you more like a colleague, a friend and a Rockstar. Not only that, but you will have a *personal* relationship at this point.

There is a significant shift in the RDM when you advance to the *support* step. When recruiters/influential individuals talk among themselves (and yes, they always are talking), they will start attaching a word with your name: Rockstar. This will add the type of excitement you want around your name and help ensure you will be selected for closed-list events and interviews.

How do I know if I have the *support* of recruiters or influential individuals?

There are many ways to tell, but you will definitely know. Some examples include when recruiters/influential individuals:

- Proactively reach out to you and encourage frank and open discussions

- Understand your special or unique concerns and provide advice

- Respond quickly and happily to requests

- Greet you by name with a strong handshake and smile—and continue to converse with you

- Share smaller details, or some personal information ("I'm from Boston, and my family loves the Red Sox!")

Once you get this far, you can almost bet you'll be a part of the interviews, as long as you actively maintain the status of Rockstar in the RDM. Keep in mind that it is possible to move backward in the relationship hierarchy; having and maintaining *support* is an ongoing process. Engage those who *support* you appropriately and don't take them for granted or overextend your position by putting them in an awkward situation. Email them only when necessary and be respectful of their time.

What's my goal when it comes to networking?

You need to advance within the *relationship hierarchy* and achieve the *support* of *recruiters* and *influential individuals* to positively impact the *recruiter's decision mindset*. However, to do this effectively, you need to understand the structure and timeline of the *MBA networking lifecycle*.

2

Now that you understand the science of networking, you need to understand how to navigate the critical first few months of business school to succeed. Hindsight is 20/20: When I look back, there are many things I wish I would have known from the beginning. The good news for you is that this chapter outlines the insights I gained since my first semester of B-school. Having a better understanding of these details will help you appropriately time your efforts and achieve your goals throughout the *MBA networking lifecycle*.

What is the MBA networking lifecycle, and what is it comprised of?

The *MBA networking lifecycle* is the period during business school in which a candidate can positively impact the RDM to receive a job offer. It begins on the first day of your MBA journey and ends when you accept a full-time offer. For some MBA students, it could begin on the first day of classes, the first day of a summer pre-program or during a summer leadership event. While the MBA networking lifecycle ends when you accept a full time offer, effective networking will be an important part of your entire career.

The MBA networking lifecycle is comprised of one-time events spanning three seasons:

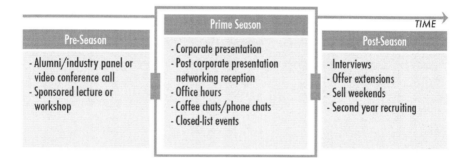

Figure 2: The MBA Networking Lifecycle

The following pages explore the events and networking etiquette for each of these seasons in more detail.

Pre-Season

I just got to campus/started my MBA adventure—what do I need to know?

For an MBA student, the pre-season may start with the first day on campus or with summer leadership programs, such as the Consortium for Graduate Studies in Management's Orientation Program and the Management Leaders for Tomorrow.

Pre-season events may include orientation panels, phone chats or workshops or lectures sponsored by a firm.

Keep in mind that these events are usually a platform for companies to showcase their brand and build relationships. Without being too pushy, you need to build *your* brand and begin to establish a position in the relationship hierarchy with influential individuals.

In the first few months of your MBA program, most firms will not expect you to know exactly why and how you are a good fit for the company. This is why firms come to campus throughout the prime season of the networking lifecycle, it gives you and them opportunities to learn more about each other on an individual basis. While *support* is your ultimate goal by the end of the networking lifecycle, the pre-season is the time to foster *awareness* and maybe *consideration*, unless you have a unique platform to really build a *personal* relationship. This is also the time for you to learn about your opportunities post-business school if you haven't decided yet.

Unique Situations

The opportunity to reach acknowledgement or support during the pre-season is rare. An example would be if a member of the firm met you at a bar after the event on a random occurrence.

In this setting, you should talk about the individual and not about recruitment. The campus event is over and the setting is informal; the last thing an influential individual will want is to talk to an overly eager recruit.

However, this is not an invitation to become "buddies." It's still important to maintain a professional demeanor. You are always being evaluated, even in casual settings.

What is the difference between firm-specific and school-specific influential individuals? How do I interact with each group?

Firm-specific influential individuals are easy to identify since they are all members of firms that will come to campus and directly influence the RDM. Outside of firm-specific influential individuals, you want to network with *school-specific influential individuals*. The pre-season is the time to focus on establishing a position in the relationship hierarchy with these school-specific influential individuals.

School-specific influential individuals fall into three broad categories: students, professors and staff. The most important of these are students, especially second-year students. This is because:

• Second-year students have lived through the first year and can provide a great deal of personal advice and recommendations on how to navigate the recruiting season with specific firms who come to your campus. Further, they can provide general guidance, such as resume feedback.

- These students may straddle the line of school-specific and firm-specific influential individuals due to their experiences and the relationships they built during their summer internships. They can provide more insight into the firm and help you advance through the relationship hierarchy with firm-specific influential individuals more quickly. Additionally, members of the firm often ask second-year students to provide feedback on candidates, which makes it important to maintain a positive rapport with second-year students.

Therefore, to fully maximize both of these benefits, your goal is to quickly advance through the relationship hierarchy with second-year students to gain their *support*. Keep in mind it is possible to move backwards in the relationship hierarchy, so carefully engage school-specific influential individuals, especially second-year students.

Keep in Mind

First-years: *Successful networking involves give and take. Second-years are still students. They also are interviewing and trying to land their dream job. Think about how your personal and professional networks can help all of your classmates.*

Second-years: *Too many second-year students dismiss first-years and don't network with them. The first-years may have contacts in their personal and professional networks that could be valuable to you. Further, supporting first years impacts both the alumni network and the school's brand.*

The financial aid director at my school knew every student. She turned out to be one of the most helpful people I knew during pre-season because she knew many alumni at my dream firm.

By advancing through the relationship hierarchy with her, I earned her support, which was evidenced by her offer to tell her contacts that she thought I was a Rockstar.

You should never underestimate who the most influential individuals can be, where they can be found and the impact they can have.

First-year students are also an important group to build a strong network with: These individuals may have worked previously with the firms in which you're interested or may know individuals who work at those firms currently. The relationships with other first-year students will be most valuable in preparing for interviews, getting valuable feedback and learning about opportunities that might interest you. After B-school, many of your classmates will move into powerful positions at some of the most sought-after companies in the world. Enjoy the journey together and establish a foundation of mutual helping that will last for the rest of your careers.

Particularly valuable resources are the student "connectors"—the first- and second-years who seem to know everyone. Get to know the connectors and ensure they understand your interests (and you understand theirs). They are a great resource to help you network with current students.

School-specific influential individuals also can be professors and staff. Professors may have working, classroom-based relationships with various firms. As such, they can introduce you to firm-specific influential individuals. In certain cases, recruiters may ask a career adviser for the names of the top students in a specific career vertical. Building a relationship with career advisers can help secure that recommendation. Furthermore, both professors and staff have developed relationships with alumni while they were students and still may keep in touch. Therefore, they may be able to influence the RDM indirectly.

In the future, you might be in a position in your career where you are looking for a different opportunity. The personal connections you make today will last throughout your lifetime and make asking for an introduction or recommendation easier.

How do I know which firms I should pursue? Is there a way to gauge fit?

First, you need to learn about the firms where you see a potential fit. Learn as much as you can about the industries in which you may be interested: go online, read articles and talk to people on campus (e.g., school-specific influential individuals) who may know about companies in those industries.

Once you better understand the companies that make sense for your career, narrow it down to the companies that really stand out. Focus on a number of companies that you feel comfortable pursuing and prioritize them. For some students, this may be one or two, and for others, it may be as many as 10 companies. Think about what is important for you as far as fit: Are you interested in constant challenge and a dynamic environment? Are you looking for a good work/life balance? Do you want a culture of entrepreneurship or a formal development model? Do you want to travel and have opportunities internationally? In addition, consider the size of the firm (as measured by the number of employees and its revenue), the locations of its offices and whether it is a business-to-business (B2B) or business-to-consumer (B2C) company. This is by no means a comprehensive list, but just a few of the characteristics you should consider when gauging how your needs and wants fit with a firm.

Remember, recruiters will come to campus to give you a chance to learn even more about the firm. By interacting with recruiters and influential individuals (and seeing how they interact with each other), you should better understand the firm's culture. Keep in mind that certain firms are quite large and have multiple smaller-scale organizations within them, which are very different from each other. For example, the finance, operations and marketing departments of a large consumer packaged goods (CPG) firm may differ vastly in how they operate, the behaviors they encourage and the type of candidate they recruit.

Once you understand the firm's culture and the attributes they are looking for in a candidate, you should craft your resume and networking approach to highlight those traits.

When is it appropriate for me to reach out to my dream firm(s) to maximize my chances of success?

Building relationships with school-specific influential individuals is important in pre-season because some firms may not participate in any sessions prior to the corporate presentation (which kicks off the prime season). If your dream firm does not participate in pre-season events, proactively reaching out to members of the firm typically is not appropriate. Allow the firm to establish a relationship and interest in you through a campus event first— then respond appropriately to positively impact the RDM.

There's a company that I'm really interested in. How important is it that I network with other companies?

It's imperative that you focus on your top choice, but it's also important to have options.

You never know what will happen—either with your situation or with the company's. Your range of options may include other firms in the same industry or another firm in a different industry of interest to you. Or perhaps you're just looking for another firm with which you think you'd have a better chance.

Your top choice may change as you learn more about the firms. While you may think initially that Firm A is where you'd like to work after graduation, you may discover that the culture at Firm B is actually a better fit.

Having options will provide you with flexibility in your decision making while still giving you the ability to adequately focus on impacting the RDM at each firm. A range of options will position you more powerfully later—even if you end up at your original first choice.

Comparing multiple companies also gives you a baseline to rank and judge what is most important to you, this is especially important for career switchers who might not have identified specific companies.

Pre-season will keep you busy with classes, new friends and new experiences, however, it is also the time to get a head start for prime season—when the real networking begins.

3

Prime Season

The corporate presentation kicks off the pivotal prime season of the MBA networking lifecycle, which is your key to success. This is your opportunity to rise to the top and stand out from your peers. It is important to remember that networking is not competitive. In-fighting between students can negatively impact both your image and your school's image. As prime season kicks off, you should be able to clearly articulate why you are a good fit for your top choices.

What is the on-campus corporate presentation, and why is it so important?

Typically an on-campus corporate presentation signals a more "official" beginning to the prime season of the networking lifecycle. The purpose of an on-campus corporate presentation is for the firm to make a formal introduction to students, usually through a slide presentation in an auditorium or large room. You'll find that the firm will bring a variety of firm-specific influential individuals, including senior partners, junior staff and the recruiting manager(s) (i.e., internal human resources staff who coordinate recruiting efforts on behalf of the firm).

The firm also may invite alumni from your school who work there or current students who interned. A good networker will find this information ahead of time and contact the appropriate individuals. That way, your in-person meeting is about putting a face to a name and makes it easier to positively impact the RDM.

My dream company is having a corporate presentation event, what should I do to prepare?

The first thing you should do is research. You will want to sound knowledgeable when asking questions about the firm and the industry. If it's your dream company, you'll probably want to do a little more research than usual, but for any company, you should at a minimum search the web for top articles on the company and skim the company's website. More research is better, but do at least the minimum so you come across as prepared.

I'm going to an event tomorrow—what should I bring?

Bring your A game!

Also, you'll want to have two pens, a pad of paper, a portfolio, five copies of your resume, a watch, gum or breath mints and business cards. If you have a card holder, bring it; if not, just have somewhere to keep them so they don't get wrinkled or ruined. Also, never chew gum in front of a recruiter or influential individual.

Business card etiquette varies by school and firm. Some might discourage the exchange of business cards, so you should abide by the standards. Further, some business schools may provide you a name tag. This should be worn on the right lapel. Recruiters typically look on your right side when they shake your hand; make it easy for them to know who you are.

Have printed copies of your resume with you because you never know when an influential individual will ask for a copy of your resume. It's not very common—but it happens. Even if you keep your resume in your portfolio sitting in your backpack on the side of the room, it's good to have it somewhere accessible instead of offering to email a copy. If you provide a hard copy, they can take a look at it right there and ask questions while you're next to them. However, keep in mind presenting your resume is only appropriate if asked specifically. Otherwise, you will risk coming across as pushy.

Even when you've provided a paper copy, you should also follow up with an email and attach your resume to provide an electronic version as well.

During the event, what should I do? How do I get noticed?

Sit in the "T-zone"—where you will be noticed. The T-zone is down the center of the room and across the front, spanning about six columns and rows.

If your event is in an auditorium where the seats get higher towards the back, then you should try to sit in the third or fourth row back, which puts you at eye level with the speaker. That way, when the speaker is looking around, he or she will look directly at you—and notice you.

While the speaker is talking, be attentive and take notes. Taking notes shows that you are interested in what the presentation is about. Keep in mind, you don't want to overdo it—don't furiously take notes and not look up!

Absolutely do not spend the presentation playing with your phone. NO EXCEPTIONS: Your phone should be off.

How should I dress for the corporate presentation?

If you're going to be noticed, then you must be worth noticing. Dressing well is important. So, what does dressed well mean? It might vary by school, but at minimum, men always will want to have a dress shirt and blazer and women will want to have a business suit.

If it's a finance presentation, men definitely should have a jacket and maybe a tie. At least bring it with you—you always want to have a tie with you. Read the situation and see if it's appropriate for the setting. I used to roll a tie and keep it in my bag. Then I'd swing down a few minutes early to see how people were dressed. Based on that, I would throw on the tie or leave it rolled in my bag. Hint: Roll the tie, don't fold it. Keep it in a resealable plastic bag in case something spills in or on your bag. The bag also prevents the fabric from getting frayed or ripped.

Women should wear corresponding business attire, such as dress pants or a skirt and a blazer or suit jacket. There is more flexibility here, but again—read the situation and dress accordingly.

As a general rule, dressing at or above the formality of the presenters/recruiters is appropriate. Also, try not to blend in. While a blazer is always recommended, try for something distinct but appropriate. It makes you more memorable. Afterwards, the influential individuals might have a conversation and try to recall you—it is helpful to call out "the one with the green scarf" or "the tall one with the brown blazer."

What kinds of questions should I ask during the corporate presentation?

Typically, you will have an opportunity to ask questions during or right after the corporate presentation. You will want to ask thoughtful questions that will benefit not just you but the others in the room. Before you ask a question, ask yourself:

- Is this relevant and interesting to the whole group?
- Will it move the conversation forward?
- If I'm asked to answer the question, do I have a perspective that I can clearly articulate and share?

If you can answer yes to those three things, then ask your question and it should be well received.

I once saw a student ask a really tough question only to have the presenter respond, "I'd love to hear your view on it first." While it was a good, challenging question, the student had not taken time to think about it himself. In addition, the question was only relevant to him, not related to the conversation and ended up being a waste of time and effort. Further, it likely negatively impacted the RDM.

Challenging questions are admirable, but remember to take the time to think about them first. Even if the presenter doesn't turn the tables on you, having at least a basic understanding of the subject will allow you to ask more thoughtful follow-up questions.

Other types of questions you should avoid in a public setting:

- Funny questions
- Calling out typos or errors on screen
- Specific questions about a practice or business area outside of the expertise of the recruiters who are present
- Overly broad questions, such as, "What are your thoughts on the current state of the economy?"

Finally, you shouldn't ask a question for the sake of asking a question—the post-corporate presentation networking event is typically the best time to get answers to your questions, especially if your questions are not relevant to the group.

4

What is the post-corporate presentation networking reception and why is it so important?

The on-campus corporate presentation typically is followed by a networking reception, which is your springboard for advancement through the relationship hierarchy with the present individuals. At the post-corporate presentation networking reception, recruiters and influential individuals will stand around the room, ready and willing to speak with interested students about themselves, their firm and the industry in general.

The networking reception is your opportunity to begin building a personal relationship with recruiters and influential individuals in a more intimate setting. You should be dressed well and prepared to positively impact the RDM by interacting with the individuals in the room.

Who should I network with at the post-corporate presentation networking reception?

Network with a variety of people, because the more people who are aware of you, the better.

The top three types of people to focus on are:

- **Recent Graduates:** These individuals are considered by the company to be closest to students. They often will spend more time with the students and give a sense of why they joined the firm, what their experience has been like and point students in the right direction for more information. These individuals are also the most likely to remember you.

- **Partners/Managers:** These are more senior individuals at the firm who have an influential say in the decision-making process. They can answer questions on firm strategy, expectations for a new hire and provide examples of thought leadership or impact of the firm's initiatives.

- **Recruiting Managers:** These are year-to-year recruiters who influence the process because they coordinate the firm's entire recruiting effort at the school. They may not be as close to the type of work you will be doing, but they know what types of candidates typically succeed.

What kinds of questions should I ask during the post-corporate presentation networking reception?

Run your questions through a mental filter similar to the three questions you should ask yourself in on-campus corporate presentations. Remember, your goal is to make a positive, lasting impression by asking smart, relevant questions about the firm, the industry and even the individual with whom you are speaking.

Here are the filter questions to ask yourself first:

- Is the question catered to the interest/experiences/background of the person with whom you're speaking?
- Is this question moving the conversation forward?
- Is the question one you really need answered at that time and in that setting?
- Can you answer the question or hold a conversation about that topic?
- Is this a unique question or a question that is asked at nearly every event?

Even if you ask a killer first question, *the real key is to listen to the response of the speaker and then ask an insightful follow-up question.* Many students tune out and begin thinking of their next question, which makes them come across as not being able to keep up an engaging conversation.

Prepare and practice a 15–30 second elevator pitch to help start off the conversation. To learn more, look to "How do I start a conversation with a stranger?" in Chapter 10: Tools & Real Examples.

What if I ask a stupid question?

Don't get stuck. It's a speed bump. Realize that it's an awkward moment, and then move right past it. You can (and need to!) salvage the influential individual's impression of you. Sometimes your mouth moves faster than your brain and you may blurt out an inappropriate or inarticulate question. Once you realize your blunder, the key question is the one you ask *after* it that leads to recovery.

For example: You shake a speaker's hand and immediately blurt out a question like, "What are your thoughts on the biggest trends in consumer packaged goods industry right now?" The speaker may think, "Whoa! Slow down!" and then respond, "That's a broad question. What exactly are you asking?"

Your initial reaction might be to think that it was a dumb question and become flustered. Instead, try to mend it. Keep your cool, and follow up with a more intelligent and clearly articulated question. You might respond with, "Well, from my previous work, I recall there was a growing trend in wellness and nutrition. What I'm interested to learn from you is what trends you see in the industry right now and how those trends impact your work."

Remain in contact and try to make a stronger impression to show that you can handle conversations (not just about CPG but also other topics) without being awkward. Basically, you're trying to work yourself out of the hole. After the event, set up time to talk again so you can continue to solidify their positive impression of you. This time, be sure to prepare (and rehearse, if necessary) intelligent questions!

How do I navigate the half-moon effect at a networking event?

In addition to the post-corporate presentation networking reception, you may attend other networking events throughout the MBA networking lifecycle. At these events, you will be exposed to the networking phenomenon known as the *half-moon effect*. The half-moon effect is pictured in figure 3.

It is characterized by a single influential individual or recruiter being surrounded by multiple students who form a half moon around him or her. This results in the speaker having to pivot and be relevant to a broad group of people. In this circumstance, the way to get noticed is to think about how you can help the speaker relate to the whole group. This includes asking smart and relevant questions, entering and exiting the half moon with finesse and positively influencing the dynamic of the half moon by reading the cues of the speaker.

Enter a half-moon when the moment is right—usually after the speaker has answered a question—and try to do so without interrupting. Then shake hands with the person you want to meet and acknowledge everyone in the half moon with your body language. Pause to see if anyone else is asking a question before asking your question.

Have a question ready. Don't go into the middle of a circle, stand there and listen to everyone else's questions and leave. This is not a good way to get noticed.

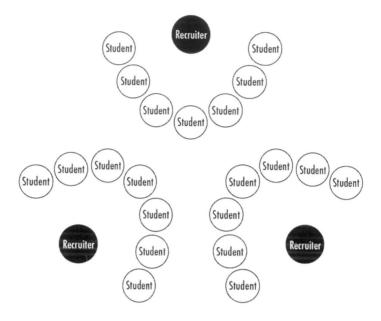

Figure 3: Half Moon Effect

Most importantly, when you ask your question, listen to the response. The real key is to listen to the response of the speaker and respond with an insightful follow-up question.

For example: You could say, "I understand you're in the consumer practice. Can you tell me about a client that you're working with right now?"

The speaker responds, "We're working with a client who works in such-and-such industry. We're working on a trade promotion strategy with this client, and we're assessing value across various vendors and distributors to see which model works best. It's a challenge because...."

If you let it die there, you will not get noticed.

You have two options to respond.

- You could say: "I once worked in a channel strategy position with ABC Bank..." and ask how they're approaching a common challenge.

- Or you could say: "I don't know much about trade promotion strategy, but I would imagine it would be difficult to try to get that information readily from all the vendors and distributors when they're also distributing other products for other companies... How do you tackle that challenge?"

Essentially, when you listen to the response of the speaker, try to find the challenge in what they're doing and ask them about that. If you're able to find that challenge and ask them questions about it, you will stand out.

This shows the speaker that you're listening, understanding, interpreting, analyzing and coming back with a clear next step of the conversation that makes him or her interested. This is how you ask Rockstar questions that make the speaker want you on his or her team.

Keeping those concepts in mind, you shouldn't be a spotlight hog. Respect your peers and also be aware of the speaker's needs—if 20 minutes go by and the speaker hasn't had a chance to get a refreshment, be keen to pick up on such things. Say something to offer the speaker a chance to step away and take a break. The key is to do it with finesse and not seem purposeful. The speaker may not take you up on the offer but will appreciate the effort.

When someone comes into your half moon, welcome them and introduce them. Even if you don't know them by name, acknowledge their entry. Once they are in the half moon, never interrupt or negatively react to another classmate. You always should collaborate with your classmates. If you don't, it will leave a bad impression on the speaker but if you do, it will look good for you and your school.

When another student enters the half moon, that's a good segue to move along. When you leave, acknowledge the speaker. Say, "It was great talking to you. I'm going to meet some of your colleagues and get some more perspective on the firm, but thank you for your time." Depending on your school culture and your comfort, asking for their business card and an opportunity to follow up with them later generally is acceptable.

Finally, it is important throughout the prime season to display strong follow-up skills. After every interaction, a thank-you email should be sent.

Post-Event Protocol

Do I need to do anything after the event is over?

Yes! You need to stand out from the crowd and differentiate yourself. Always leave time after an event for follow up—even if it means delaying dinner.

First, you should jot down notes or interesting things from each person you spoke to. Then draft *personal* follow-up emails to each of those people—hopefully reminding them of the memorable conversation you had with them. You can find sample emails in Chapter 10: Tools & Real Examples.

Finally, for the ones you felt a closer relationship with—that is, those with whom you hit it off—request a follow-up conversation. Hopefully, this list will include a majority of the members present. You also can leverage this group of people to get in touch with any other members of the firm whom you did not get to meet.

When should I send the follow-up email/note?

You should send a thank you email as soon as possible and definitely within 24 hours of the event for the most impact. Ideally, you would send a thank-you email one to two hours after the event is over. Make it obvious that you took time to think about your message.

Never send the email between 10 p.m. and 7 a.m. Here's why: Everyone you will meet will probably have a smart phone, which alerts them if they have a new message. If you email them during the night, they will wake up and see an email from an eager recruit, which will not leave a strong, positive impression.

Further, sending a hand-written thank you note is well-received, but not required. This note should be a sincere message that highlights a positive impression you had of the firm and/or individual and your enthusiasm to learn more.

What are best practices when it comes to thank-you emails/notes?

Your emails should be short and concise. Again, this is due to the manner in which influential individuals will receive the email—they're most likely reading it on their smart phone.

Tailor your emails and hand-written notes based on your conversation to personalize it—do not copy and paste the same message to multiple members of the same firm. They will know it was not genuine when they compare notes (and they will!). Some firms share all candidate communications with the entire recruiting team. When all emails from a candidate start and end the same way, it's clear that the student didn't take the time to connect personally with the specific recruiter.

For the first round of emails/notes, you should keep the tone formal. It's a mistake to be too informal on the first email/note you send. Don't assume that you can be very conversational, even if you feel that you built a positive relationship. Let the influential individual respond back casually, then you can adjust accordingly.

Don't send an unnecessarily long email/note and assume you have an understanding of the job and the skills that are necessary—this typically is viewed negatively. Instead, send a concise and genuine note, requesting additional time for a phone call. Sell yourself on the phone, not via email/note. If you're wondering what a good email or note looks like, you can find examples in Chapter 10: Tools & Real Examples.

OK, so I've sent my thank-you emails/notes, what do I do next to get that interview?

Between the on-campus corporate presentation and the first-round interviews, the firm typically will hold formal coffee chats and office-hour sessions to really get to know you. At the same time, this is your opportunity to build personal relationships with influential individuals through your conversations.

Consider prime season as an open invitation for you to request (typically via email) additional time to chat with influential individuals on the phone. These phone conversations are primarily for you to advance your knowledge of the firm, but more importantly are a one-on-one opportunity to advance further in the relationship hierarchy.

During these chats, you need to convey that you are a strong fit for the firm and have the attributes that are important for the positions in which you are interested. Before engaging in one-on-one conversation, either in person or by phone, read Chapter 9: Self Assessment & Determining Fit to better understand your strengths and weaknesses across the list of Rockstar attributes, how to understand which attributes are important to your dream firm(s) and how to best communicate the fit between the two.

5

One-on-One Conversations: In Person

Office Hours/Coffee Chats: These are just relaxed conversations, right?

No, think of this as your first interview. The recruiter is taking valuable time to meet you and your classmates. The coffee might be good, but they are more interested in determining whether you would be a worthwhile candidate.

Your goal is to put your best foot forward so they realize that you are a Rockstar. The chat might seem laid-back, but it is evaluative. Be prepared for anything—even a case or a scenario to see how you problem solve or manage situations.

Take it seriously and maybe even prepare for some light interview-style questions, though it will vary from firm to firm. Typically, it is less formal than an interview.

Focus the conversation on the top two or three things you are interested in knowing—not on a laundry list of items. Also, link the conversation to your background and your fit with the firm.

Consider these discussions an opportunity to ask smart questions and advance through the relationship hierarchy. Before speaking, run your questions through the same filter as the networking reception questions. Ask yourself first:

- Is the question catered to the interest/experiences/background of the person with whom you're speaking?

- Is this question moving the conversation forward?

- Do you really need the question answered at that time and in that setting?

- Can you answer the question or hold a conversation about that topic?

- Is this a unique question or a question that is asked a thousand times?

Remember, even if you ask a killer first question, the real key is to listen to the response and then ask an insightful follow-up question. This will lead to a conversation that will positively impact the RDM.

What is the recruiter trying to ascertain in the conversation? How should I approach it?

The recruiters want to know if you are a good fit for the firm. They want to find out what you would be like to work with and how interested you really are. Some of the questions they may ask themselves during the chat include:

- Would I want to work with you? Do you pass the airport test? That is, if we were stranded together at an airport, how would it be?

- Do you have the skill sets needed to succeed at the job?

- Do you have relevant experience?

- Are you motivated and engaging?

- Do you seem ethical and trustworthy?

- Are you truly interested in the firm or just shopping around?

- In what area/department/role in the firm might you fit well?

Properly conveying your fit with the attributes of a candidate that a firm values is paramount to a successful interaction.

What if the chat goes horribly wrong?

If you think that the conversation didn't go well and you negatively influenced the RDM, you should talk to a second-year student who knows the firm and get feedback and advice. You might need to immediately address the issue after the chat via email and if appropriate, or you might want to set up a call to discuss it.

Another option is to follow up with another member of the firm with whom you have a stronger relationship. Mention to this person that the chat didn't go well—it's probably not necessary to give specific details—and ask them for suggestions on how to improve the situation.

There is no clear method of handling this type of situation, but a second-year student can act as your best guide in navigating it.

This advice also applies when one-on-one conversations by phone don't go as planned.

One-on-One Conversations: By Phone

As mentioned earlier, you can consider prime season to be an open invitation to request additional time on the phone with influential individuals to advance your knowledge of the firm and more importantly, advance in the relationship hierarchy on a one-on-one basis.

I got a positive response to my request for a follow-up phone call! What do I talk about?

Before you make the call, figure out what your goal is. You will want to have that influential individual know more about you in a context that is relevant to the job. You want to communicate that you are a good fit and have the proper attributes that the firm values. Most likely, you will express interest in the company and will want to know more about its day-to-day work. Prepare your questions around your goal.

Don't forget—you're not the only one calling them. Most of your classmates are doing the same thing, as are candidates from other schools. Although you may have met the individual before, be wary of assuming he or she remembers you—reintroduce yourself at the beginning of the call. By the end of the call if you're able to leave a lasting impression, you'll stand out.

How long should the call be?

The call should be about 10 to 15 minutes and certainly no more than 20 minutes. Respect their time, even if it's going well. Asking at the 15-minute mark if you can continue with one or two more questions also is a good idea.

If you have more questions or would like to continue the conversation beyond that time, ask if they have more time or if you could set up another time to speak later. Certain individuals might really enjoy the conversation and continue to speak with you beyond 15 minutes—as long as the recruiter or influential individual is willing to extend the conversation, you should continue as well.

What are some best practices for the call?

Before you begin the call, make sure you're in a quiet location with no distractions or background noise. Be ready five minutes early and write out your agenda and/or questions. Have a glass of water nearby in case your throat gets dry. If you're calling from a cell phone, make sure you have a strong phone signal.

Take some deep breaths and try not to get overly anxious. Begin the call by introducing yourself and asking if it's still a good time to speak. It's possible that the influential individual is working with a new project deadline, caught in traffic, running late, etc.

From there, verbally outline an agenda and objectives for the call. For example, you might say, "Thank you for taking the time to speak with me. On today's call, I would like to tell you about myself and understand more about your experience with the firm. Specifically, I have questions around X, Y and Z."

During the call, communicate clearly and concisely. You will benefit by giving the influential individual an opportunity to tell you more about the firm and their background. Don't spend a majority of the call on one topic. Take the opportunity to cover a breadth of information.

As stated earlier, ask relevant and thoughtful follow-up questions. Do not make the call an interview where you ask a question and listen to answers. If you don't tie the conversation and questions to your background, strengths and/or weaknesses, then the call will be a lost cause. Remember, you want to advance through the relationship hierarchy with that influential individual to positively impact the RDM. This call is a key indicator the influential individual will use to decide if you would be a good fit at this firm.

If an emergency arises and you're going to be late for the call, let the person know as soon as you can—at least 10 minutes before the call via email. Ask if you can call five minutes after your initial start time or if rescheduling is better. Apologize for the inconvenience and reinforce the message that the call is very important to you and that you very much value their time. When you finally have the call, thank them for being flexible with their time.

How do I end the call?

Keep track of the agreed upon time (usually approximately 15 minutes). As that time approaches, acknowledge it by saying that you realize their time is valuable and that you very much enjoyed the conversation (hopefully you did!). If they are able to continue the conversation, keep going.

If the conversation must end, thank them and ask any necessary follow-up questions: Can we set up time in a few weeks to speak again? Can you direct me to someone who can talk to me more about subject X?

Is it OK to discuss off-topic items?

It can be. You're building a personal relationship by advancing through the relationship hierarchy. You can have a great talk about golf and still succeed.

If you try to talk about "the game last night" or an off-topic item— be careful. It can come across as not very genuine and a waste of time. Read the situation and base your approach on previous interactions with that influential individual. If you learned last time he or she has a newborn baby, you could ask, "How's little Matt doing?" (Remembering the baby's name will score you some serious points!) If you talk about an off-topic item, keep it brief and let the influential individual show interest before continuing on the topic.

If it goes well, it's acceptable to continue for a while. However, even if the conversation goes off-topic you should be mindful of the time allotted. And, most importantly, ensure your questions about the firm are answered and that your interest is noted. At the end of the chat, ask to set up a follow-up call if you did not get to accomplish the goals you outlined for the call.

What should I do after the call?

Send an email, following the same guidelines as you did with the email following a corporate presentation.

Send the email within 24 hours and not between 10 p.m. and 7 a.m. since he or she most likely will receive an alert on his or her smart phone.

> **Tip:**
>
> *A good way to enhance a relationship is to leverage the opportunity to ask for feedback on your resume or any aspect that might help you succeed.*

What if I've already waited too long to follow up after the call?

Send an email or note now. It's better to send it late than not to follow up at all. If it's been very long, you might want to apologize and acknowledge the delay.

You never want to let a relationship die. Even if you decide to pursue another firm or hit it off with another individual, you should always maintain the relationships you start during the MBA networking lifecycle.

What if I didn't get a positive response to my request for a follow-up phone call?

If you sent an email requesting additional time but haven't gotten a response at all, keep in mind that the person might be busy. Reach out to them again after one or two weeks, but don't be overly pushy. If you still don't get a satisfactory response, then consider reaching out to your other contacts within that company.

Another option is to follow up with another member of the firm with whom you have a stronger relationship. Mention to this person that you tried to reach out to a specific person but have not gotten a response and are very interested in talking with this person. Ask your other contact what you should do.

6

Closed-List Events

Prime season may include a closed-list event, which is vitally important to ensure you are selected for interviews.

I got invited to a closed-list event! What do I do? How do I prepare?

Congratulations! This is a clear sign that the firm is interested in you. An invitation means you are a top candidate for an interview offer. It also indicates that you successfully advanced through the relationship hierarchy with influential individuals.

Before the event, go through your notes, review the list of people you've spoken to and also refresh yourself on any research you did. Reach out to those influential individuals with whom you've built good relationships. Tell them that you're excited to attend the event and are looking forward to seeing them again if they are attending.

I didn't get invited to a closed-list event. What do I do?

If you didn't get invited, you need to realize that the recruiters put you into a maybe or no bucket. The best thing to do now is to use this as a learning experience. Reach out to influential individuals with whom you've built a close relationship. Reiterate your continued interest in the firm, mention your disappointment in not being invited and request feedback about how you can improve. While you still might not get an invite, they will note your strong, genuine interest in both the firm and in your personal growth. They might be able to help you understand where you need to improve for next year. It is likely that a company will turn you down, so don't take it personally. You can use this feedback to improve your chances of success with the remaining companies on your target list.

Keep your relationships open with recruiters and influential individuals if it doesn't work out for you—you can always go back to them for full-time recruiting support during your second year.

Note:

Some firms might not provide feedback from interviews, so do not take it personally if you are unable to receive feedback from recruiters or influential individuals in the firm. In such circumstances, if you have built a strong personal relationship, you might receive some informal feedback on your candidacy.

What's my goal when attending a closed-list event?

Closed list events exist for firms to better understand your fit. If you are invited, it means recruiters and influential individuals see potential in you and that you successfully networked to build personal relationships with members of the firm. Other candidates at this event are also seen as "high-potential" candidates, so you need to stand out and continue to build personal relationships.

Overall, you have three goals:

1. **Continue to advance through the relationship hierarchy by speaking to as many people as possible.** Once again, networking is not a numbers game, but about establishing new relationships or strengthening already existing ones. If you recognize individuals with whom you have built a relationship, seek them out first and solidify their view of you as a Rockstar. Then ask them for advice on who else you should make a point of meeting at the event. They will at least let you know which practices/departments each recruiter or influential individual is from. If you have their support, they might even directly introduce you. Typically invitations for interviews are discussed after the event by the entire team, so if people leave the event without having any idea who you are, they are less likely to be convinced by others that you are a Rockstar candidate. Maximize your exposure—show up on time and move around the room having meaningful, but short, conversations to advance through the relationship hierarchy.

2. **Positively impact the RDM by clearly articulating why you are a strong candidate.** With every conversation, clearly articulate your attributes that make you a strong fit for the firm. If the firm values analytical skills, bring up examples from your past that show you can navigate analytical tools very well. If it's a marketing firm, bring up examples of from your past that are relevant (e.g. "Before B-school, I worked with the marketing department to launch a new product and learned a lot from that experience.")

3. **Reiterate your strong interest in the firm.** Remember, while you might have amazing experience and be a strong fit with the attributes the firm seeks, they want to know you are excited to join their firm! If you come across as disingenuous, uninterested or name-drop other firms you're in contact with, it doesn't come across as very professional and can hurt your candidacy. Convey your interest in the firm with excitement and show that you've done your research. For example, you can mention a new product, publication, invention or innovation that directly influences the firm's work.

What are the next steps once the event is over?

Before leaving the event, thank everyone you spoke with and compliment them with genuine thoughts on the event (for example, you could say, "It was great being able to speak to members of your firm in such a nice, intimate environment.").

Once again, follow the same guidelines as you did with sending the email after a corporate presentation. Send the email within 24 hours and not between 10 p.m. and 7 a.m. since they're most likely going to receive an alert on their smart phones.

Post Season

If you are successful in positively impacting the RDM during the prime season, you likely will play an active part in post season—as an interview candidate! Firms usually have two rounds of interviews, with only a fraction of the first round interviewers passing onto the second. Of these, a select few will be given offers.

If you make it to the post season, your competition is among the best of the best. It will end one of two ways for you: either with or without an offer. Depending on your outcome, the post season is an enjoyable experience where the firm focuses efforts on ensuring you accept the offer or it becomes a long extension of prime season until second-year recruiting begins. If you're in the latter group, the good news is you can leverage your experience of this year for more success next year.

I got an interview! What do I do?

Congratulations! Reach out to those in your network, thanking them for all their support and reiterating your excitement to have been selected to interview. Ask them for advice on the interview process as they can be instrumental in helping you understand what is required to get the offer.

Hopefully, this book has helped you achieve your goal of being selected for an interview. Now you need to showcase your strengths and fit for the position(s) for which you have been selected. Continue to focus on your interview and case prep (as applicable). Other books target these specific areas. Good luck!

I didn't get an interview. What do I do?

Of course, not everyone will be selected for an interview in the post season. This could be the result of not having the right fit, or not properly conveying fit through effective networking. Use this as a learning experience. Reach out to individuals with whom you've built a close relationship and mention your disappointment in not being invited and request feedback. They might be able to help you understand where you need to improve.

Hopefully, you have been networking with other companies, so focus your efforts on the other remaining companies. Try to learn what you might have done wrong and leverage these lessons to succeed with your other target companies.

7

OFF-CAMPUS NETWORKING & EVENTS

Not all companies recruit at all campuses. You may have identified a firm that you believe is a good fit for your skills and your interests, but this firm might not recruit at your school. In this case, you will have to work harder and smarter to network effectively with recruiters or influential individuals who can help you get an interview and an offer with your dream firm.

What if my dream firm does not recruit on campus?

If your dream firm does not recruit on your campus, it likely recruits at a set of "core" schools and is less interested in hiring candidates from "non-core" schools. However, there are still ways to get noticed by these firms. When you get an opportunity to interact, make a powerful, positive impact and quickly build a personal connection to gain their *support*.

An effective way to get noticed by influential individuals or recruiters at these firms is to build awareness through direct or indirect channels. As you expand your network, you may realize that someone you know has a contact at your dream firm. If you have a personal connection and have this individual's support he or she will likely refer you to someone at the company who can directly influence your chances of getting an interview.

If you do not have anyone in your network who can help, try other methods, such as leveraging your alumni network, cold-calling potential contacts and/or attending national networking events.

How do I leverage my alumni network or "cold-call" potential contacts at my dream firm?

Alumni networks can be very powerful. You may find that an alumnus of your B-school or an earlier school you attended, such as your undergraduate university, works for your dream firm. While you have a strong context of reaching out to the individual since you both attended the same school, you should not assume that the alumnus is already in your personal network. Rather than sending an email asking for a reference, reach out to the alumnus to set up a call. You may want to indicate that you are interested in the firm, that you are eager to learn why the individual joined that firm and what the experience has been like so far. An alumnus more likely will respond directly to a request for a call to learn more about his or her journey and experience than to respond to a reference request from someone they don't know personally.

For samples of how to request time through "cold-calling," please see Chapter 10: Tools & Real Examples.

You have three main goals for the call:

- Connect with the contact to show how your skills and attributes fit those the firm seeks.

- Ask for feedback on your candidacy and your fit with the firm.

- Ask for help with next steps (e.g., an introduction to either a recruiter or influential individual in the firm).

Further, go online and research various articles or reports published by or about members of your dream firm. For example, if you read an exciting article that provides the author's contact information, you can reach out to that individual telling them you enjoyed reading the article and what you thought was interesting about it. If you are able to connect with this person, use the opportunity to ask smart questions to engage him or her in a professional conversation. During the call, mention your background and interest in the work— then work to accomplish the three goals mentioned above to proceed through the relationship hierarchy.

Cold-calling is potentially the most dangerous way to connect with your dream firm. Remember, the note you send will be unsolicited, so the person to whom you are sending it might react adversely or may simply ignore your request. Since you represent not only yourself, but also your school, you need to be extremely professional. The person you reach out to may not be able to help you directly, but could help introduce you to someone who can.

What are national networking events, and how can they help me get my dream job?

Multiple off-campus networking events or career fairs are held throughout the season providing you with the opportunity to meet a large number of recruiters and influential individuals from a multitude of firms. Be prepared to meet them in a fast-paced, high-pressure setting that will provide you with only a small window of opportunity to build a personal connection. Networking fairs combine many of the elements in this book from cold-calling to navigating the half-moon effect. Reading this entire book will help prepare you for almost anything that happens at a networking event.

National networking events range from the small (a series of invitation-only networking receptions or pre-selected interviews from resume screens) to the large (a huge room with a multiple booths with recruiters and influential individuals ready to shake hands and meet you). Smaller events are like the closed-list events discussed in Chapter 6, while the larger events are similar to the post-corporate presentation networking events highlighted in Chapter 4. When researching the event, look at the schedule of events to get a better sense of what to expect. Certain events may have speakers or panels that can give you additional exposure to recruiters or influential individuals from your dream firm(s).

Keep in Mind

National industry meetings or tradeshows are also a great way to get exposure to certain firms, even though these events are not recruiting specific. You can still network with representatives of your dream firm in a less formal setting.

Regardless of the format, networking events are an opportunity for you to get exposure to firms you are interested in whether or not they recruit on your campus. The more exposure you have to a firm, the better opportunity you have to advance through the relationship hierarchy with multiple individuals to positively impact the RDM.

I'm going to attend a networking event—what do I need to know?

You need to know how to maximize your time and effort to achieve your desired outcome. Before heading to the event, find out what the format of the event will be, then create a plan that answers the following eight questions:

1. **Have I done enough research on the firm(s) I am most interested in that will be at the event?** You can expect to be very busy at the event, so prepare as much as you can beforehand. Learn as much as you can about every company with which you anticipate networking and make a one page reference sheet for each that has key points. Keep these sheets with you and review them before meeting with members of the firm. Networking events can be very tiring, and it is easy to forget names of people with whom you spoke or the specifics of an article you read. You don't want to come across as if you haven't done any research or mistakenly confuse companies and seem as though you are not genuinely interested or dedicated to a firm. The more you know about a firm beforehand, the better positioned you will be to network with the full list of companies you are targeting.

2. **Which companies am I targeting?** A lot of companies will be in attendance, so focus on your key firms, but be open to learning about the others. Typically, a list of the participating companies (and contact information) will be available online beforehand. If available, you should reach out to any contacts before the event with a concise email introducing yourself, explaining your fit and interest in the firm, stating that you are looking forward to meeting in person and with your resume attached for reference. Most networking events have an online system or protocol for sharing this information ahead of time.

3. **How do I prioritize my efforts with each firm?** Even after you've selected your key companies, you still might need to trade off which company's event you attend if they are at the same time. You need to prioritize your company list and have a clear idea of how you will make quick decisions in the moment. Remember, your prioritization might change as you meet various people and learn more about the firms. Your prioritization should be based on your interest, fit with the firm, your chances of success and potential opportunities to meet with the company in a different setting.

4. **Did I assess how well I fit with each firm?** During your research, determine which skills and attributes are important to each firm and why the firm would be interested in you. Once you determine what the firm seeks in a future employee, you will have a better idea of how to stand out among hundreds or even thousands of candidates by demonstrating the strengths you have that match the attributes the firm values.

Keep in Mind

At the end of the conference, recruiters will have stacks of resumes/contacts that will be placed into four piles: yes, no, maybe and Rockstar.

5. **How will I convey my strengths and weaknesses along the set of attributes that the firm(s) seeks?** Think of strong examples of what you've done well and show self-awareness that you've come to B-school to learn how to fill the "gaps" in your story. Refer to Chapter 9 to better understand how to assess fit and strengths across various attributes that are important to your dream firm(s) and how to best convey your strengths and address your weaknesses. By creating a compelling story, you can positively impact the RDM in a short time.

6. **What's my elevator pitch?** Create a 15- to 30-second elevator pitch that:

   • Shows who you are and illustrates your interesting/relevant background

   • Explains why you are interested in the firm

   • Demonstrates why you are a good fit

   Since you will have such limited exposure to recruiters or influential individuals, it needs to be short and punchy to get the attention of the various people with whom you will network. You might even slightly change your elevator pitch depending on the firm/industry.

7. **Am I fully aware and signed-up for the massive amounts of follow-up required?** You probably will send hundreds of follow-up emails. You need to be organized and should keep a running list of who you spoke to and what you spoke about. You will have to send follow-up emails immediately after interactions—copying/pasting will get you into a lot of trouble. You want to stand out by being concise and meaningful in your wording and having tailored the email to the individual to whom it is addressed. The challenge will be managing all of the information and tasks while running to and from events. Additionally, you may need to be more aggressive/adamant due to the "short exposure" nature of such events.

8. **What is my exit strategy?** If you get stuck in an event or conversation you want to end, how will you end it to move to the next person/event? You need to thank people for their time, exchange business cards and follow-up. Even if you don't immediately think there is a long-term potential, show respect by following up appropriately. If you decide not to pursue an opportunity after the event is over, communicate that later. (Remember, you might change your mind or your circumstances might change.) Don't let any relationship die. Recruiters and influential individuals you meet might be able to help you in an unexpected way or you might be able to help a classmate with your newly expanded network.

Finally, remember: Dress to impress and smile to succeed!

8

SECURING THE INTERNSHIP OR FULL-TIME OFFER

I got an internship offer! What do I do?

Congratulations! Reach out to those in your network and thank them for their support and reiterate your excitement to have the offer. More than likely, they will contact you to congratulate you on your achievement.

Carefully review the details of the offer and write down any questions. As individuals reach out to you, start getting answers to your questions so that you can make an informed decision. If you have multiple offers, you may mention this in conversation—but do not lie or intentionally mislead one firm about the offer of another. If a contact at one firm asks you about the details of another firm's offer, you can say you don't feel comfortable sharing specific details such as compensation.

You may, however, want to share basic information about your offers. If you received multiple offers, each firm likely will want to know which other firms gave you an offer, the office locations and the practice/department. Such information will help companies shape their interactions with you and understand what is important to you. Of course, each firm will want you to accept their offer—you need to take the opportunity to get all of your questions answered and learn more about your fit with each firm to make the best decision for your career.

Once you decide to accept an offer, tell the other firms who also gave you an offer. Keep communication open with these contacts. They want you in their firm now, so they will likely consider you in the future.

I didn't get an internship offer. What do I do?

If you were invited to interview, but unable to secure an internship offer, you should try to find out why by requesting some feedback. Certain firms will be more open to sharing feedback, while others may have a policy against it.

Begin by engaging the right people at the firm and acknowledge the situation. Make them aware that you are open to feedback and willing to amend anything you may have done that hurt your chances with the company. Show that you are interested in developing personally and are dedicated to enhancing your skills to improve your chances of being a candidate for a full-time position. The feedback loop can be very valuable.

Real-Life Example

I really wanted to work for Company A, but they didn't interview me the first year. I networked with many individuals from that company, but realized I never got past consideration or acknowledgement with any of them. (An aha! moment for me.)

When Company A made their interview announcement and I was not selected, I sought feedback from them. After that conversation, the recruiter saw that I actually might be a good fit—even though I didn't look good on paper or do a good job of impacting the RDM by advancing through the relationship hierarchy with influential individuals from that company. He provided some great feedback and told me to touch base with him after my summer internship to see how I developed against the feedback he provided.

I interned with Company B, a firm similar to Company A. I gained tremendous experience and development. At the end of the summer, I contacted the recruiter from Company A and discussed my experience. Since I had a strong personal relationship with him and showed him that I genuinely was interested in the firm and willing to put forth the effort, he became my supporter. I also engaged another influential individual in Company A—a second year student who had accepted his full-time offer with Company A. By advancing through the relationship hierarchy with this individual, he also became my supporter and I was included in the second-year full-time interview list.

I have been wait-listed, what do I do?

At times, a firm may be interested in you but cannot or will not make you an offer immediately. There are a few reasons for this. The company's executives may not be sure of its needs/capacity over the summer, or they may have made offers to other candidates and are waiting to hear back from them before making you an offer.

Being wait-listed is a delicate position. You should reach out to your network and show the same enthusiasm and dedication you would show had you been given an offer. Reiterate your excitement to join the firm and communicate your eagerness to be moved from the wait list to being extended an offer. If you built a personal connection and have the *support* of certain individuals you may ask what you can do to improve your chances.

If you are on a wait-list, you are already viewed as a strong candidate. Typically the decision to extend the offer is dependent on the circumstances mentioned earlier, so your best bet is to maintain strong communication with the firm that made you an offer. At the same time, knowing that you may not actually get an offer, focus your attention on securing an offer with another company.

Finally, consider macroeconomic factors. If the job market is good, you may have the upper hand since companies will fight for top talent. If the economy is weak, it's less likely that a wait-list will turn into an offer. Either way, you need to keep your options open and ensure that you have a strong summer experience to help you achieve your career goals.

I am a student trying to secure a full-time offer with a firm I'm interested in but wasn't successful with previously. What do I do and when?

If you did not advance to the post-season in your first year of B-school, you need to understand your situation better by using the seven-step process below as a guide:

1. Send personal emails to one to three recruiters/influential individuals from the firm to request feedback as appropriate. Typically, a good group of individuals to whom to reach out are recruiting alumni. These are alumni from your school who are actively engaged in the recruiting process for their companies. You should reach out to *at least* three individuals, which will strengthen your foothold in the company and also protect you against any potential staffing changes (e.g., someone leaves the firm). Additionally, you also will receive more varied feedback to help you improve when you reach out to multiple sources. Some firms do not allow their employees to give feedback, so do not be discouraged if you do not get the response you would like.

2. Engage these recruiters/influential individuals in conversations where you clearly state your enthusiasm and dedication to the firm and specifically request feedback on your resume and your candidacy. End the conversation with a list of improvement objectives and timeline for reconnecting.

3. Lock in a good internship that will be a beneficial experience for you. Hopefully, you have been networking with several companies, so focus on solidifying a strong summer internship opportunity with your other target firms.

4. Send an update to those people in your network midway through your internship highlighting your progress against your improvement objectives. Also, include additional details about what you learned from your experience (e.g., "I've really learned a lot about marketing strategy.").

5. At the end of your summer internship, include these newly acquired skills and experiences on your resume. Align your new functional skills/experiences to those that your dream firm specifically seeks.

6. Two weeks before school starts, send an email to all of your contacts at your dream firm. Don't copy and paste the same email to everyone. Update them briefly on your summer experience, attach your resume and request some time to chat with them on the phone. Let them know how you've progressed against the feedback they provided and what you've done specifically to address the concerns shared with you.

7. Follow through with a phone conversation and be confident (but not cocky) about your development over the summer. Reiterate your interest and dedication to the firm and ask for continued guidance and feedback on how to improve your chances of securing an interview in your second year. Express interest in interviewing again and ask for advice on how to best position yourself to be considered this time.

Reach out to multiple influential individuals and enhance your relationship with them. Clarify you are very interested in the firm. Be adamant. The worst the company can say is no again. Be careful, however, not to be too pushy or unprofessional. You are not only representing yourself, but also your school.

Follow up with your classmates who interned with that firm over the summer or reach out to last year's second-year students who now work there full time. Hopefully, these are influential individuals with whom you already have built a strong personal relationship. Keep in mind, most firms fill their hiring quota through summer internships and may vary in terms of how many additional candidates (if any) they will recruit in the fall for full-time positions.

Finally, re-read this book for advice you may have missed the first time or that can be useful again moving forward.

9

SELF ASSESSMENT & DETERMINING FIT

What attributes are recruiters really looking for in a Rockstar candidate?

Recruiters need to feel confident that you are a Rockstar. In order to do so, they will try to understand your performance against educational benchmarks, the characteristics of your work history and the skills you garnered through your experiences both in and out of the workplace.

When it comes to your performance against educational benchmarks, recruiters will look for strong numbers, including your GPA and your performance on standardized tests, such as the GMAT. Additionally, they will assess the academic rigor of the institutions you attended and the coursework you have completed. Finally, they will look for your involvement in clubs and activities available at your business school that are relevant to the position for which they are recruiting.

The characteristics of your work history will give recruiters a better understanding of your story. They will look for a logical progression and examples of advancement/promotions. They also will look for how lengthy and varied your work history is. In addition, they will look if you worked with a recognizable company or brand name, which lends credibility to your experience and gives recruiters a better sense of your story.

The most important attribute that recruiters typically look for in a Rockstar candidate are strong skill sets that are relevant to the position. Some of the questions they might ask themselves include:

- What leadership skills has the candidate demonstrated?

- Does the candidate have analytical/modeling experience?

- Has the candidate demonstrated innovative thinking?

- Does the candidate have experience communicating with a range of audiences, including senior executives?

- Has the candidate successfully worked with a team to accomplish a goal?

- What activities has the candidate participated in outside of work and what skills were learned or demonstrated?

Recruiters will look at your story not in pieces but as a sum of its parts. You do not necessarily need to surpass all educational benchmarks, display amazing work history characteristics and demonstrate strengths in all relevant skill sets. Even though you may not have strengths in every attribute (especially on paper), you still can be a Rockstar by networking effectively.

How do these attributes vary by firm? How do I ensure I properly project my fit with the relevant attributes?

Doing your homework about the firms in which you are interested is very important. The recruiters and influential individuals are doing their homework by trying to get to know you better. Start by understanding what attributes the firm values, then you more masterfully can communicate and showcase those traits on your resume and in conversation.

While it is safe to assume that all firms would like to recruit the Rockstar candidate who has all of the attributes listed in the previous question as strengths, the reality is that some of those attributes will not relate directly to the work you will need to do. This is why networking can be so powerful.

For example, if you do not have the best performance against educational benchmarks, but the skills sets you have garnered through your experiences are the perfect match for a firm, then you are more likely to be considered a Rockstar candidate. Performance against educational benchmarks is just one indicator of your potential success with the firm. While the entire list of attributes helps paint a full story about a candidate, certain firms definitely will hone in on the aspects they find most important to the work you will be expected to perform in the positions for which they are recruiting.

Marketing firms will stress good communication and innovative thinking while finance firms will stress analytical ability and evidence of ethical decision-making. However, there is no one formula for fit—it depends on the industry, the company, the department and sometimes the office in which you are interested. Do your homework early and engage with your dream firm through the networking lifecycle, and you will understand better which attributes they value.

Your goal is to communicate your fit with the relevant attributes through your resume and the various interactions you have with recruiters and influential individuals throughout the networking lifecycle. Some of these attributes may be your strengths while others may be a weakness. Still, you can convey a more complete story of your fit with the firm by assessing yourself against these attributes and networking effectively.

How can I assess how strong/weak I am across this list of attributes?

The first thing to keep in mind when self-assessing across this list of attributes is that there is no one profile for a Rockstar. Various combinations of strengths and weaknesses are in high demand and highly respected in the industry.

The charts that follow contain examples of what are typically considered strong and weak across this list of attributes to give you a better sense of how your background stacks up. There is no official rating, but use these benchmarks as a guide to understanding where you stand. Further, once you complete this exercise, gauge your relative competitiveness against your classmates.

EDUCATIONAL BENCHMARKS		
ATTRIBUTE	EXAMPLE OF STRONG	EXAMPLE OF WEAK
Relevant scores/ numbers	• GPA above 3.5 • Graduated in top percentile/ with honors (summa cum laude, magna cum laude, cum laude) • GMAT in high 700s	• GPA below 3.0 • Graduated without distinction • GMAT below 650
Rigor of institution	• Attended a top-ranked school with a well-recognized academic history	• Attended a lesser-known college or university with limited recognition of strong academic history
Rigor of coursework	• Coursework that combines core relevant skills such as math, science and communication, e.g., engineering, marketing analytics, computer science and biology/chemistry	• Coursework that excludes one or more of the core relevant skills in favor of a non-core skill, e.g., theater, dance, history and language arts
Recognition and involvement in relevant clubs, activities and programs	• Scholarships/Fellowships clearly articulated on resume • Membership or leadership position in relevant clubs, e.g., interested in consulting and has joined the consulting club	• No or non-communicated scholarships/ fellowships, i.e., missing from resume • Involvement in non-relevant clubs, e.g., interested in consulting, but member of finance club • No or non-communicated involvement in relevant club, e.g., interested in consulting but consulting club not listed on resume

WORK HISTORY CHARACTERISTICS		
ATTRIBUTE	EXAMPLE OF STRONG	EXAMPLE OF WEAK
Logical progression/ advancement	• Started in an entry-level post-undergrad position relevant to coursework and shows evidence of promotion quicker than regular cycle	• Started in an entry-level post-undergrad position not relevant to coursework • Non-intuitive lateral jumps across non-related industries • Little to no evidence of advancement/ promotion
Length and variety of work experience	• Five or more years of experience with one or more related companies in a certain industry or related industries • Evidence of involvement with challenging projects across a variety of roles	• Less than one year of experience • Long gaps between new roles and responsibilities • Little variance in roles and responsibilities
Recognizable brand name	• Worked directly or indirectly with a recognizable brand name company or product, e.g., experience with GE, which consistently is named one of the top companies that produces strong leaders	• Worked with smaller or lesser-known companies whose development model or culture/ expectations are hard to assess

SKILL SETS/ EXPERIENCES		
ATTRIBUTE	EXAMPLE OF STRONG	EXAMPLE OF WEAK
Leadership	• *Clearly exhibits multiple examples of successfully leading teams and/or projects* • *Recognition/awards for leadership both in and out of the workplace*	• *Limited or no examples of exhibited leadership* • *Examples of leadership that are examples of performing work responsibilities well but are not leadership, e.g., auditor states that she worked to resolve a financial gap in a client's account*
Analytics/ modeling	• *Demonstrates mastery of Excel and/or other analytical tools in problem solving* • *Has used modeling/ analytics to deliver substantial results/ savings to the company*	• *No or limited familiarity of Excel or other analytical tools* • *Limited use of modeling/ analytics to deliver results/ savings to the company*
Innovative thinking	• *Clearly exhibits multiple examples of suggesting innovative ideas that were implemented* • *Recognition/awards for innovation both in and out of the workplace*	• *Limited or no examples of innovative thinking* • *Examples of innovation that are not truly innovative or are logical conclusions as the result of a study (examples and interpretations can vary)*
Experience	• *Clearly exhibits multiple examples of communicating with and persuading diverse audiences, including top executives, to adopt an idea or to gain buy-in*	• *Limited or no examples of communicating with and persuading diverse audiences, including top executives, to adopt an idea or gain buy-in*

SKILL SETS/ EXPERIENCES		
ATTRIBUTE	EXAMPLE OF STRONG	EXAMPLE OF WEAK
Worked with a team to accomplish a goal	• Led a large, diverse and/ or multi-functional team to accomplish a goal, overcoming significant challenges	• Limited or no examples of teamwork or people/ project management • Examples of teamwork that accomplished a goal with little to no significant challenges
Non-work activities that demonstrate new skills	• Well-rounded character, showing interest in non-intuitive fields, for example, poetry, choreography or skydiving • Examples of leadership in community involvement resulting in significant differentiated impact	• Limited creativity or challenge in fields of interest, e.g., reading and watching TV • Examples of leadership that are basic participation in community service organizations

What can I do to positively impact my networking goals if I find one of these attributes to be my strength?

Ensure that recruiters are aware of your strengths without coming across as overly confident or deserving. Try not to come across as if you are bragging or name-dropping. Certain information is best communicated through a resume, not in conversation. A recruiter typically will make a decision based on your whole story, not just because of one name on your resume or because you started a successful non-profit organization.

Understand the culture of the firm in which you're interested. For example, if it's collaborative, highlight examples from your background in conversation to show that you can fit in culturally with the firm of your choice. If it's an analytics-driven firm, then highlight modeling and analytic experience from your background.

Make your complete story available. If recruiters only see one part of your story consistently—even if it's a good part—they won't be able to make a decision regarding your candidacy based on your other attributes that make up the full story.

Example: Not Communicating Your Whole Story

Peter is an MBA student who had a fairly lengthy and varied work experience in sales and found it easy to advance through the relationship hierarchy. He seemed like a great candidate on paper, so Alex the recruiter was looking forward to meeting him in person. Alex knew Peter had strengths in communication, but wanted to ensure Peter also could handle the analytical or modeling aspects of the job description. More importantly, Alex wanted to assess Peter's fit with the firm's culture. In conversation, Peter emphasized his strengths and came across as if he was trying to "sell" Alex. Peter failed as a candidate to communicate in person his analytical abilities and fit with the firm beyond his out-going personality. Alex only experienced one aspect of Peter's full story and walked away from the conversations believing that Peter was not a well-rounded Rockstar.

In this scenario, Peter would have been more successful if he had been aware of which strengths had already been communicated through his resume and interactions so far and which weaknesses he needed to address through conversation. By failing to communicate effectively his other strengths in various attributes, he did not provide Alex with a complete story to positively impact the RDM.

What can I do to positively impact my networking goals if I find one of these attributes to be a weakness?

While recruiters will be aware of your strengths either through your resume or through conversing with you, they also will question perceived gaps in your story. Limited strengths in the attributes of a Rockstar candidate are only weaknesses if you let them be.

Sometimes your weaknesses can become your greatest strengths. Yes, recruiters will discuss gaps in your story, but this active discussion gives you a platform to show how you are improving against those perceived gaps. The following three examples provide a more clear picture of how weaknesses can be leveraged as strengths.

Example: Questionable Analytical Abilities

Sally the student was a journalism major who had a strong GPA and performed well on the GMAT. She was interested in a marketing analytics advisory firm. As a journalist, she clearly had strengths in communication but not many examples of analytics or modeling in her background. Sally selected a business school that was known for a quantitative focus. When interacting with recruiters and influential individuals, she made a point to remark that the marketing analytics class was extremely interesting to her because she had not had much exposure to analytical tools before. She further remarked that she was doing well in the class and thoroughly enjoyed the prospect of performing such work as a career. Sally successfully leveraged a clear gap in her story by highlighting that she was aware of it and actively addressing it. She gave recruiters a more complete picture of her story and now only needed to ensure she exhibited her newly learned analytical skills during the interview process.

Example: Short/Non-Relevant Work History

Casey the candidate was a double major in biology and math. For the last five years, he worked in research and development for a pharmaceutical company. He now wanted to pursue a career in management consulting. His coursework and academic scores showed he had the analytic abilities to solve difficult problems, but communication skills seemed to form a gap in his story. To show that he did have strong communication skills, Casey listed his involvement in Toastmasters on his resume and discussed how the skills required to pitch a product idea to senior executives for research support were similar to those required to make a final consulting recommendation. Even though he didn't propose complicated strategies to senior executives in his past, he learned the specific tact, approach and considerations required to gain buy-in from senior executives.

Example: Low GMAT scores

Gary the graduate student had a decent undergrad GPA, but a weak GMAT. Gary was an engineer who worked in operations and wanted to pursue a career in operations consulting. Many firms liked his background, but found it odd that none of his scores were listed on his resume. He was diligent in building personal relationships with multiple recruiters and influential individuals throughout the networking lifecycle to showcase his abilities, knowledge and fit with the firm(s) in which he was interested. Once he built a personal relationship, he leveraged the recruiter as a mentor/advocate and asked if the non-listed scores would pose an issue for him to work at that company. Since he already had reached the level of support within the relationship hierarchy, the recruiter shared with him that the scores are a benchmark for them to consider candidates; however, having gotten to know him, the recruiter felt confident that Gary would be able to meet the requirements of the job. The GMAT score was only a number, and only one part of Gary's whole story.

There are different ways to communicate your story—sometimes telling a recruiter or influential individual isn't enough; you need to show them that you possess a skill or understand the unique attributes required to succeed. A good way to do this is to bring in specific examples of what you have learned from your prior experiences. Remember, instead of listing your skills—either on your resume or in conversation—try to bring them to life by showcasing outcomes or evidence of development.

10

TOOLS & REAL EXAMPLES

With an understanding of the science of networking, how to navigate the MBA networking lifecycle and how to assess yourself against a series of attributes that firms value, you should be set up for success. However, taking the principles of this book and using them in practice is challenging for many students.

This section provides you with additional tools and real examples of how to leverage the lessons of this book to succeed in your networking. Each example has an analysis of what makes it good or bad. You shouldn't follow these examples verbatim—use them as a reference to give you insight into what kinds of conversations and interactions students have with recruiters. This section should dispel some of the mystery of what students think they're *supposed* to do to network effectively for success.

How do I start a conversation with a complete stranger?

Easy. All it takes is three simple words. When I want to start a conversation with someone I don't know, I extend my hand for a handshake, and say, "Hi, I'm Jaymin."

This initially may feel unnatural, but the first thing you must do to start a conversation with a complete stranger is introduce yourself. Many first-year MBA students will try to be creative or differentiated and risk over-thinking their introductions. But no matter who you are, you can always strike up a conversation using those three simple words.

It's not always easy to start a conversation with a stranger if there's no context for you to engage them. The strangers you meet on campus will be recruiters or influential individuals who will positively impact your career trajectory. Therefore, you have that context to reach out to them to strike up a conversation.

It's very easy to feel intimidated with the prospect of having to speak to very influential and accomplished individuals. You are in business school to enhance your career. Remember, you were accepted into your MBA program because someone thinks you are an accomplished individual—so go out there and prove that you are!

Everyone with whom you interact has the potential to be that key person who leads you to the success you seek. While more obvious influential individuals can be found on your campus throughout the networking lifecycle, you may even find that you benefit most from conversing with the person seated next to you on an airplane. However, in the context of an airplane, you may want to take it down a level and first say, "Hi, how's it going?" before introducing yourself.

The three-word introduction is very powerful—just try it. You can try it at the bar on the weekends, at a coffee shop or at a networking event. No matter when or where you try it, I'm confident that the other person will shake your hand and introduce themselves, too.

Once you get the introduction out of the way, you need to focus on the conversation. All you need to do is continue it. Many students may get flustered thinking of what comes next. You have two options:

- Provide more context about yourself. Begin by preparing and practicing an articulate 15- to 30-second elevator pitch, which concisely demonstrates who you are and why you are talking to this stranger. For example:

  > **Student**: Hi, I'm Ashley.
  >
  > **Recruiter**: Hi, Ashley, I'm Mark.
  >
  > **Ashley**: Great to meet you, Mark. I'm interested in learning more about the financial services practice in your firm. I have a background in trading and am pursuing my MBA to transition into an advisory role.
  >
  > **Mark**: Oh, that's great. That's exactly the type of background that we typically look for. What would you like to know about our FS practice?
  >
  > **Ashley**: Well, can you start by telling me more about the work that you do?
  >
  > Conversation continues...

- Ask an immediate question to begin the dialogue that is relevant to the individual with whom you are speaking. Throughout the conversation, deliver your elevator pitch. For example:

  Student: Hi, I'm Ashley.

  Recruiter: Hi, Ashley, I'm Mark.

  Ashley: Great to meet you, Mark. I'm interested in learning more about the financial services practice in your firm. Can you tell me more about the work that you do?

  Mark: Yes, definitely. I work in the financial services practice and focus most of my time in international markets.

  Ashley: Wow, that's exciting. I actually have a background in trading and am pursuing my MBA to transition into an advisory role.

  Mark: Oh, that's great. That's exactly the type of background that we typically look for.

  Ashley: Can you tell me more about the FS practice?

  Conversation continues...

Ultimately, the conversation covers the same ground, but the approach is different. Find which approach works best for you and leverage that approach to build rapport with the recruiter/influential individual with whom you are speaking.

Note: Even if the person does not align with your interests directly, you should leverage the opportunity to learn about the individual and the work that they do. This is a good opportunity to learn about the firm, build a connection and ask for a referral to someone who does the work that interests you.

When approaching a stranger to strike up a conversation, you need to read and respond to his body language. If he is welcoming, smiling and has high energy, then engage him at that energy level. Conversely, don't be deterred if he doesn't react to you in the positive way you were anticipating. Simply adjust your energy levels and slowly bring his energy up. Get him excited to talk to you, but be aware if you're about to overstep a boundary. Some ways to tell that he's not interested in speaking with you include him moving his eyes away from you, physically stepping away from you or seeming as though he's not fully engaged in the conversation. While there are many reasons why this might happen, you should read the situation and politely end the conversation if necessary.

Be aware of your own body language as well. You should have good posture and your body should be open to the individual with whom you are speaking. Make eye contact, smile and project positive energy. Avoid slouching, looking disinterested or preoccupied by glancing around the room as if planning your next steps.

How do I reach out to individuals who are not in my personal network (cold-calling)?

Keep in mind when reaching out to these individuals that your request is unsolicited and possibly unexpected. You must maintain a professional and respectful tone and not be overly pushy or aggressive. See the following pages for an example of this type of email.

Sent: Mon, 4/18, 8:03 pm

From: Valerie Banner

To: Tom Kolla

Subject: Request From Valerie Banner, First-Year MBA at ABC Business

Dear Mr. Kolla,

Good afternoon! I am Valerie Banner, a first year student at ABC Business School. I obtained your contact information from the school alumni database.

I am writing to you today because I am interested in learning more about you and your experience at ACME Company. I have researched ACME Company and am very impressed by the portfolio of products it markets, the development opportunities available to new associates and its reputation for innovative thinking.

I have a background in supply-chain operations and worked extensively with the marketing department at XYZ Company to support a national launch of a new product. I believe marketing can be a good career fit for me and chose ABC School because of its strong reputation in this area.

I would like to request 10-15 minutes of your time to learn more about your experience at ACME via a phone call. I understand you have a busy schedule, and I very much appreciate both your time and consideration.

I have attached my resume for your review and look forward to hearing back from you soon.

Best Regards,

Valerie Banner

Analysis of Unsolicited Email to an Alumnus

√ *Formal opening*

√ *Starts with brief introduction and explanation as to how she received his contact information*

√ *Briefly explains why she's reaching out and lists what qualities she likes best about the company*

√ *Shows evidence that she has done her research and is not just "shopping around"*

√ *Gives a short overview of her background and experiences to show why she could be a strong candidate*

√ *Respectfully requests time for a phone call*

√ *Is conscious of the time involved*

√ *Indicates resume is attached for more information and gently sets an expectation to hear back soon*

√ *Formal closing*

Sent: Mon, 4/19, 6:04 pm

From: Monica Jain
To: Tom Kolla
Subject: Request From Monica Jain, First-Year MBA at ABC Business

Dear Mr. Kolla,

Good afternoon! I am Monica Jain, a first year student at ABC Business School. I recently read your article on new consumer trends impacting the marketing of durable goods and found it very fascinating. I especially agreed with your view that consumers are becoming more cost conscious, which creates a challenge for marketing firms in educating customers about the quality of products to increase their willingness to pay.

I am writing to you today because I am interested in learning more about you and your experience at ACME Company. I have researched ACME Company and am very impressed by the portfolio of products it markets, the development opportunities available to new associates and its reputation for innovative thinking.

I have a background in supply-chain operations and worked extensively with the marketing department at XYZ Company to support a national launch of a new product. I believe marketing can be a good career fit for me and chose ABC School because of its strong reputation in this area.

I would like to request 10-15 minutes of your time to learn more about your experience at ACME via a phone call. I understand you have a busy schedule, and I very much appreciate both your time and consideration.

I have attached my resume for your review and look forward to hearing back from you soon.

Best Regards,

Monica Jain

Analysis of Unsolicited Email to Someone Not in Your Personal Network

√ *Formal opening*

√ *Starts with brief introduction and explanation as to how she received his contact information*

√ *Discusses a topic important to Mr. Kolla (his paper) and presents her views on the paper to illustrate her knowledge of the topic, without coming across as disingenuous or pushy*

√ *Briefly explains why she's reaching out and lists what qualities she likes best about the company*

√ *Shows evidence that she has done her research and is not just "shopping around"*

√ *Gives a short overview of her background and experiences to show why she could be a strong candidate*

√ *Respectfully requests time for a phone call*

√ *Is conscious of the time involved*

√ *Indicates resume is attached for more information and gently sets an expectation to hear back soon*

√ *Formal closing*

If you do not receive a response (positive or negative), it's acceptable (and sometimes appreciated) to be adamant and send a follow-up note the Monday after the first full week that passes after sending the note. If you still do not receive a response, you probably should move on to other potential contacts.

How personal should I get while networking?

Always err on the side of keeping your relationships professional versus personal. The recruiter or influential individual always takes the lead in indicating what level in the relationship hierarchy he or she views you to be. Getting personal while networking depends on the relationship between you and the recruiter/influential individual. For example, always compose emails with a formal title. If the individual responds signing their first name or a shortened version of their name (e.g., Liz rather than Elizabeth), then you may address your next email to "Liz."

In conversation, you need to pick up on these cues more quickly. Below is an example conversation in which Matt the candidate is speaking to Jose the recent alumni/recruiter.

Matt: So, Jose, I understand you are in the Boston office. Why did you pick that office?

Jose: Well, I had a choice between two offices and my wife got a job here, so I decided to move to Boston.

Matt: It's definitely a great city; had you spent much time there before?

Jose: Yes, actually, my wife and I met here, and both my kids were born here.

Matt: That's fantastic. I don't have any kids of my own, but I have two young nephews who I adore. Are your kids very young?

Jose: They are 4 and 6, and they are both Red Sox fans.

Matt: I hope the team does well this year. My nephews are 5 and 8, and they're both Cubs fans. It's definitely a great age. I love being able to see them.

Jose: Yes, I agree. We'll have to keep up with each other about how well both teams do this season.

Notice Matt starts with a broad question that is professional but could lead to a personal answer

Jose divulges some personal information to Matt in his answer

Matt wants to play it safe, so he asks a similarly broad question that Jose could answer either personally or professionally

Jose provides some more personal information, feeling comfortable in his conversation with Matt.

Matt decides to offer some of his own personal information, which relates to Jose's personal information. He also reads the situation and decides to ask a personal question.

Jose answers his personal question and provides more information, indicating that he is comfortable with this level of conversation.

Matt again divulges personal information trying to better relate to Jose. Instead of asking a question, he makes a statement to see how Jose will react.

Jose reacts positively and invites him to a more personal connection that they can share regarding baseball throughout the season.

Within one conversation, Matt was able to reach the level of *acknowledgement* with Jose. Jose more than likely will recognize Matt the next time they meet—the conversation will not only be about Jose's firm, but will be about baseball and his children. Matt seems to have established the beginning of a personal relationship with Jose. By continuing this trajectory carefully, Matt may gain Jose's *support*.

What should a thank-you email/note look like?

Thank-you emails and notes need to be sincere. They also must be personal, so copying and pasting the same email/text to multiple recipients does more damage than good. Recruiters will know the note is not personal and that you sent the same email/note verbatim to other co-workers. On the following pages are some examples of good and bad emails. Rather than focusing on the example itself, try to understand the analysis portion, which breaks down the positive and negative attributes of the email/note.

Keep in mind there is no one format of a letter that is perfectly good or bad. When composing your thank-you letters, consider the context in which you are sending the note. Think about the following questions:

- Did you háve a memorable conversation when you met?

- Did you make a positive impression in that meeting?

- Do you feel you have a strong personal connection?

- What is the perceived style of the person to whom you are sending the note?

- What is the perceived culture of the firm?

Based on your answers to these questions, you may deem attaching your resume, including additional talking points or adjusting the formality of the note appropriate.

The samples that follow are just examples to display the characteristics of good and bad thank-you notes. Rather than using the wording in the notes as a template, focus on the characteristics in the analysis portion as items to keep in mind when writing your thank-you emails/notes.

Sent: Wed, 4/21, 1:14 am

From: Mamta Doshi
To: Jaymin Patel
Subject: Hey!!

Hey Jaymin!

Wanted to thank you for coming to campus and discussing your experience with ACME Company. I really enjoyed learning from you of your expereince.

I think I have the background and qualifications to be successful at ACME company. I'm a good leader, communi9cate well and am always smiling -just ask my last boss!

Anyways, I would love to learn more about your company in the coming months and look forward to seeing you around. I am usually available on Mondays and Wednesdays before 12, or on tuesday and thursday after 3:30. I can also take a call on Friday, usually between 2-4, depending on my study group. Of course, if you cant make that time, then I can adjust my schedule if that works for you. I am attending a wedding this weekend, so besides that, just let me know. We can speak for maybe 30 minutes, if that works for you? Just let me know, it can be shorter or longer if you want!

Take it easy this weekend!

Mamta

Analysis of a Poorly Written Email

√ *Sent at a late hour*

√ *Introduction is not formal enough*

√ *Has spelling/grammar mistakes throughout (e.g., "communi9cate")*

√ *Does not differentiate who she is by referring back to an earlier conversation*

√ *Candidate already feels qualified for position without having a real opportunity to learn about it—very presumptuous*

√ *Sentences are too long*

√ *Way too conversational—leave some for the phone*

√ *Request is confusing and inarticulate*

√ *Closing is too informal*

Sent: Wed, 4/21, 12:43 am

From: setharoo123489@email.com
To: Jaymin Patel
Subject: Thanks

Jaymin,

Thank you for coming to campus and speaking with us about ACME company. I enjoyed learning about your firm and look forward to more opportunities to interact.

Sincerely,

Seth

Analysis of a Poorly Written Email

√ *Very short, impersonal email—a recruiter/influential individual can tell no thought was put into it*

√ *Differing fonts make it seem like it was copied and pasted*

√ *Poor ending—no action item/follow up requested. Lets the relationship die*

Sent: Wed, 4/21, 2:55 pm

From: Corey Judson
To: Jaymin Patel
Subject: Thank you

Dear Jaymin,

Thank you so much for coming to campus today to discuss ACME Company. I enjoyed meeting you and learning more about your experience in the financial sector. I found it especially helpful to hear about your experiences in the firm when you interned as an MBA student in Tokyo.

I am very interested in pursuing a summer internship opportunity with the firm and would like to request 15-20 minutes of your time to ask some follow-up questions and learn more about ACME.

Please suggest a time that is convenient for you in the coming weeks as I can adjust my schedule. Thank you again, Jaymin. I look forward to speaking with you soon.

Best,

Corey Judson

Analysis of a Well Written Email

√ *Formal opening*

√ *Starts by thanking the recruiter*

√ *Shows enthusiasm about aspects of the firm/recruiter/ conversation that he enjoyed*

√ *Outlines specific points that were discussed to help the recruiter recall the conversation*

√ *Succinct, yet warm communication*

√ *Clear and specific request*

√ *Shows flexibility to the busy recruiter's schedule and asks for an action.*

√ *Personally thanks the recruiter by name and shows excitement for the next opportunity to connect*

√ *Formal closing*

How should a one-on-one phone conversation flow?

Again, there is no formula that outlines the perfect conversation; however, here are some additional examples and analysis to help you understand best practices.

Sample Conversation

Christian: Hello. Thank you for taking my call. Is this still a good time?

Yu: Yes, it's definitely a good time.

Christian: Fantastic, thanks again, so how are you doing? How's your project going?

Yu: Good, I'm in Chicago right now. We're going to be wrapping up the project in two weeks.

Christian: Have you been able to take time to enjoy the city? I love visiting my family in Chicago. One of my favorite things is going to see The Bean with my family.

Yu: Oh no, I haven't had much free time. I haven't checked out The Bean but I'll be sure to.

Analysis

Christian, the student, checks if Yu, the consultant, still has time for a focused and meaningful call

Christian thanks Yu and asks a conversational question to see how she responds

Christian gets city information, so he tries to relate his experience of being there and brings in some specifics (e.g., The Bean, a Chicago landmark)

Yu shows some interest in the specifics, which Christian introduces into the conversation

Christian: Definitely, I'll email you some info about it. I think it's really cool. So anyway, we have about 15 minutes for the call, I would like to learn a little bit more about your story with ACME Firm and why you chose it, what the culture is like and hear your advice on what I can do in my first year to prepare for the recruiting season.

Christian finds something informal that he can follow-up with—this can help lead to a more personal relationship

Christian brings the call back on task, recognizing Yu's time is valuable. He goes on to lay out a clear agenda of what he would like to accomplish in the allotted time

Yu: OK, sounds great.

Conversation continues...

Thanks Yu in non-generic fashion (e.g., insightful)

Christian: Thanks so much. These answers have been very insightful. We're approaching the 15-minute mark, but before we end the call, I wanted to know if you could put me in touch with someone who is from the financial services practice so I can learn more about it.

Stays aware of time and shows he appreciates the limited time he was allotted for the call

Clearly requests next steps

Yu responds positively

Yu: Sure, please send me an email to remind me.

Christian thanks Yu again and outlines what will happen next

Christian: Definitely, thank you so much. I appreciate your help. I'll send you a reminder. Have a good night—and don't forget to check out The Bean.

Christian ends the call by touching on a non-work related topic introduced earlier in the call

NOTE: If you say during the call that you're going to follow up with an email afterwards, make sure you do so within 24 hours. It should be clear and to the point and include all the relevant information you discussed. For example, a follow-up email to the above conversation would include a reminder about getting in touch with someone from financial services and a quick note about The Bean.

What should my communications look like if I am invited to an event, interview, etc.?

Thank everybody for their support through the recruiting season and clearly show your enthusiasm and that you appreciate being invited. Thank those with whom you've connected for their support. Do not copy and paste the same email to everyone.

See the following pages for an example of this type of email.

What should my communications look like if I am *not* invited an event, interview, etc.?

Although not being invited to an event or interview can be an emotional experience, the letter should be rational and straightforward. It should have a professional air but be written personally to each individual you are contacting—do not copy and paste.

See the following pages for an example of this type of email.

Sent: Wed, 4/21, 7:25 pm

From: Dia Jones
To: Amit Shah
Subject: Thank You - From Dia Jones

Dear Amit,

Hope you are enjoying your time in Chicago and your project is going well. I just received notification that I have been selected for the closed list event. I am very excited to be included in this select group and have the opportunity to interact more closely with members of your firm. Thank you so much for all of your support thus far in the recruiting cycle.

Will you be attending the event? If so, I look forward to seeing you in person. Additionally, if you have any advice/insight on how I can best prepare for the event, I would really appreciate it.

Thank you,

Dia

Analysis of an Email Sent After Receiving an Invitation to an Event or Interview

√ *Opens with a personal note*

√ *Shows genuine enthusiasm and excitement for the event, without overdoing it*

√ *Shows appreciation to the influence Amit has had in the decision to invite her*

√ *Connects on a personal level and indicates excitement to further build the personal connection to two share*

√ *Asks for advice on how to be successful in the event, without making a specific request for a follow-up*

Sent: Wed, 4/21, 7:25 pm

From: Dia Jones
To: Amit Shah
Subject: Thank You and Request for Feedback

Dear Amit,

Hope you are enjoying your time in Chicago and your project is going well. Recently, invitations were sent out to students for the closed list event. Unfortunately, I was not one of the students selected. I am extremely interested in ACME Company and am dedicated to pursuing available opportunities with the company.

I know you are quite busy, but I would appreciate any guidance or feedback you can provide so that I can improve my chances of success with ACME. I believe this feedback can help me become more self-aware and help me improve both professionally and personally.

Please let me know a time that is convenient for you, and I will adjust my schedule accordingly. Very much looking forward to speaking with you soon.

Best,

Dia

Analysis of an Email Sent After Not Being Invited to an Event or Interview

√ *Opens with a personal note*

√ *Clearly lays out the actions/issues*

√ *Reiterates interest and dedication to ACME specifically*

√ *Recognizes the realities/limitations of the request*

√ *Seeks practical guidance/feedback— NOT an invitation*

√ *Shows that she wants to improve from the experience*

√ *Requests a clear action item for follow-up*

√ *Demonstrates willingness to prioritize ACME (values the company)*

√ *Hints at wanting to connect quickly and that time is of the essence*

I am a student trying to secure a full-time offer with a firm I'm interested in but wasn't successful with previously. What should my communications look like?

Follow a seven-step process similar to that outlined at the end of Chapter 8: Securing the Internship or Full-Time Offer. For specific examples of the emails referenced in these steps, see the pages that follow.

- **Step 1:** Send personal emails to multiple recruiters/influential individuals from the firm to request feedback.

- **Step 2:** Engage these recruiters/influential individuals in conversations

- **Step 3:** Lock in a good internship that will be a beneficial experience for you.

- **Step 4:** Send an update to your network midway through your internship.

- **Step 5:** At the end of your summer internship, update your resume to include newly acquired skills and experiences.

- **Step 6:** Two weeks before school starts, send an email to all of your contacts at your dream firm with a request for conversation and with your updated resume attached for reference. Don't copy and paste the same email to everyone.

- **Step 7:** Follow through with a phone conversation and clearly articulate your development over the summer with confidence. Reiterate your interest and dedication to the firm and ask for guidance/feedback on how to improve your chances of securing an interview in your second year.

Sent: Wed, 4/21, 7:25 pm

From: Adi Desai
To: Anand Shah
Subject: Thank You and Request for Feedback

Dear Anand,

Hope you are well. I am very interested and dedicated to pursuing an opportunity with ACME; however, I was not selected for an internship offer this year. I am very interested in developing both personally and professionally and would appreciate some pointed feedback on how I can improve my candidacy with ACME between now and full-time recruiting next year.

I understand your time is valuable, and would truly appreciate having a 10-15 minute conversation where we can discuss feedback on my candidacy.

Thank you again for your continued support.

Best,

Adi

Analysis of an Email Sent to Recruiters/Influential Individuals to Request Feedback (Step 1)

√ *Formal opening*

√ *Reiterates interest and dedication to firm*

√ *States that despite not being selected, she is interested in developing personally and professionally*

√ *Clearly states request for feedback to improve candidacy*

√ *Recognizes that the time is valuable, and requests only a short amount of time*

√ *Professional closing*

Sample Conversation (Step 2)

Adi: Hello! Thank you so much for taking the time to provide me with feedback. I am extremely interested and dedicated to pursing an opportunity with ACME and would appreciate any guidance or feedback you can give me on my resume or my candidacy.

Anand: Sure, let's begin with your resume and then get into some more specific feedback.

They review resume and discuss feedback and improvement objectives.

Anand: I think this was a really good conversation. I've been able to learn more about you. If you improve on the specific things we've talked about, I think we would consider you for a full-time position next year.

Adi: Thank you so much. I learned a lot from the call. I will check in with you halfway through my internship and will set up a call with you toward the beginning of my second year.

Analysis

Adi thanks Anand for his time

Adi reiterates interest/ dedication to the firm

Clearly requests feedback on resume and candidacy

Adi is able to communicate a more complete story to Anand in the one-one-one interaction

Adi highlights that she learned from the call and is eager to improve

Adi clearly lays out next steps

Anand: Great. I wish you success in your summer experience and look forward to hearing from you.

Adi: Thank you again for your time. I truly appreciate it.

Adi ends the conversation with a sincere thank you

Sent: Wed, 8/27, 3:28 pm

From: Adi Desai
To: Anand Shah
Subject: Summer Follow Up From Adi

Dear Anand,

I hope you have enjoyed your summer. I definitely have. Working for Smith Associates has been a fantastic opportunity to not only learn more about the industry, but also to improve against the feedback you provided to me in May. I've attached an updated resume to highlight some newly acquired skills and experiences and would love to discuss this further with you.

Please let me know a time that works best for you to connect. I am looking forward to speaking with you soon.

Best,
Adi

Analysis of an Email Sent After Summer Internship (Step 6)

√ *Opens with a personal note and shows increased confidence from the summer experience—in effort to intrigue Anand*

√ *Clearly articulates her experience in learning about the industry and her development against her specific improvement objective*

√ *Has attached her resume for Anand and requests a conversation*

√ *Indicates her excitement to connect*

11

BEING YOU!
HOW TO STAY GENUINE
WHILE NETWORKING LIKE A ROCKSTAR

This book contains numerous examples and best practices to guide you in how to network effectively. To succeed, let your personality shine through and take it to the next level.

The tools and lessons in this book can help you gain confidence, take smart actions, avoid common mistakes and get noticed in the right way by the right people throughout the MBA networking lifecycle. However, you must remain genuine in your interactions and show dedication to the firm(s) in which you are interested. Once you get an interview, you will need to further showcase your skills and abilities to actually get the offer!

There are three steps to success:

1. **Find balance:** Be confident in your actions and take the proper steps necessary to get noticed by recruiters; however, you need to add your own touch of personality. There's no right mix: You've made it this far in the process, and now with the right tools at your disposal, you need to find the balance in what works for you and what doesn't. This book showcases many examples of good and bad, but there are other approaches that work. If it doesn't feel natural, find what works for you. No matter what route you take, create and market your own brand to the firms in which you are interested. Also, you need to find balance in the effort you put into networking—it's very easy to stretch yourself too thin. Prioritize your dream firms and appropriately spend time networking with the ones that are most important. In addition, balance your time between networking with firms and preparing for interviews in the post season.

2. **Practice:** You might not feel sure about how all the pieces fall together or have the confidence to try something different. But remember: Practice makes perfect. The more you perform an un-natural activity, the more comfortable you will be with it moving forward. Once you have practiced various approaches and found the one with which you are most comfortable, add your own spice to build your confidence and really make it work for you!

3. **Fail faster:** Nobody plans for failure. You probably bought this book to keep from failing! However, the key to success is to learn how to fail faster and in a low-risk setting. Try an approach and test it out in different scenarios. Push yourself

out of your comfort zone in a setting that isn't as high-risk as a post-corporate presentation networking event. Failure is an incredible learning tool—it helps you understand and really analyze your actions. If you try various strategies with friends or with strangers, you can get feedback and improve for important networking situations.

Ultimately, you are a Rockstar candidate already—now you have the tools and knowledge to network effectively and be successful!

Epilogue

NETWORKING FOR A LIFETIME
BY: SUBU NARAYANAN

Networking doesn't end with getting the job. Networking is among the most important tools for success even after you have your dream job. Like it or not, the knowledge and education that you have accumulated thus far in your career is only a small portion of the information you will need for success in the workplace. Knowing how to access that additional information—and making sure that it is the right information—can be difficult. This is where networking, once again, comes into play.

A quality network will give you access to the relevant additional information you need. There is a lot of information out there, but much of it is irrelevant. What sets the Rockstars apart from the average performers is their ability to access the right information, faster. How do they do it? They reach into their network!

This is not a trivial matter. The quality of your network can mean the difference between bagging a critical deal or losing an M&A opportunity. It can mean the difference between budget approval for your dream project or having your initiative shot down. Thinking back to my sales days, some of the most critical negotiations that I won were due to my ability to reach out to the right people in my personal network. Whether it was obtaining a commitment for a tight delivery deadline quicker than my competition or connecting a customer to the right industry expert, my strong network was the secret to my success.

Though my experience happens to have been in sales, I believe this is relevant across the business spectrum. I learned this lesson early in my career, and it helped shape my approach as I grew and held various positions—I always made networking a priority. Thus, I firmly believe that it is critical to continue building and strengthening your network throughout both your personal and professional life.

Networking is more than just tooling around with social networking sites or attending a work happy hour. It's more than just asking a favor from a friend or contacting a previous employer for a letter of recommendation. Rockstars approach networking in a very diligent and deliberate manner. Jaymin summarizes this idea when he writes, "Effective networking is more than just getting exposure, it involves learning who the right people are, when to interact with them, and how to interact with them [...]." This statement is worth elaborating on beyond the recruiting aspect.

Beyond initial exposure

It is not enough to just know of someone. Networking is about developing personal relationships with people. You can consider someone a part of your network only if you are able to pick up the phone and talk to them or send them an email and get a quick response.

The right people

A useful and resourceful network is not something that can be built in a day. In order to know—and be able to find—the right people, you need to start building your network now. Building and adding to your network is a continuous process—do it when you don't need it and it will help you in your time of dire need. Spend time identifying critical individuals around you and build relationships with them. Identify how their positions, interests or knowledge align with your interests and aspirations. These individuals will be able to refer you to others in their networks, who, in turn, will eventually expand your network. Through this thought and practice you will easily be able to access the "right" people when you need them.

When to interact

Networking is not a one-way transfer of information. Being a good network citizen involves giving as much as taking. You need to be willing to invest time and be a resource to others. To be able to do this, you should build up your area of expertise. As a tenured partner at McKinsey & Company told me when I was a young associate: "Know something about something." Build a niche and be known for something. Whether it is something as technical as lean operations or as artful as knowing where to find the best restaurants in the city; as long as you are a wealth of knowledge in one area, people are going to use you as a resource. This is the formula for being a successful network citizen. This will help enable others in your network to identify you as the "right" person, as well.

How to interact

Not only do you need to be able to successfully identify the right people, but you also need to know how. It is essential to follow the basic etiquettes of networking:

- **Be polite when asking for information**: Relevant information is not a freely available commodity. People build their expertise and reputation in an area over a period of time. Being polite while asking for information is akin to giving respect to that time, effort and knowledge. News about impolite or rude behavior may pass very quickly within the network and can negatively impact you.

- **Respect people's time**: Do not demand responses or set strict deadlines while asking for information. Similar to the points made above, this shows that you value their time and understand that they may have other deadlines to meet.

- **Always thank and give credit where due**: Email or call and thank the person for the information provided. It is always useful to follow up and share any key insights from your work, which may be useful for the person to add to his/her knowledge base.

Networking is something you naturally take part in, perhaps, without even realizing it. Networking is an extension of the socializing that you do in everyday life. My sister used her network to determine which school to enroll her kids. My mother uses her network to get the best shopping deals from the streets of Mumbai. In this book, Jaymin details how he used his networking skills to get interview opportunities at several leading companies. Think of networking as a more diligent and thoughtful way of socializing.

With some understanding of the art and science of networking as outlined in this book, you will be well on your way to not only your dream job, but a very rewarding post-MBA career!

Subu is an MBA graduate of the Tepper School of Business at Carnegie Mellon University and is currently employed at McKinsey & Company.

Note

A NOTE TO PART-TIME STUDENTS:
YOU GOTTA WORK HARDER!
BY: MANEESHA MUKHI

Recruiting for full-time job opportunities on campus is particularly challenging if you are a part-time student. The objective of this note is not to discourage you from recruiting, but to inform you of the challenges that lie ahead so that you are able to prepare for them appropriately. There are numerous hurdles that you will have to cross to make it to the interview process with a desired firm.

Know the facts

The rules around part-time student participation in recruiting vary across schools, so first and foremost, gather the facts around the prerequisites. Most schools require part-time students to complete 10 to 12 classes before recruiting season. Depending on when you joined the part-time program, you may hit that target at a regular pace or you may have to speed up/slow down your classes. Plan carefully so that you meet this requirement before the fall of the season you would like to recruit for.

Start early

Full-time students are exposed to recruiting and networking almost immediately upon entering an MBA program. On the other hand, part-time students enter the MBA program at various times of the year, and often aren't in sync with the recruiting cycle.

Do not wait until the summer before recruiting season to start networking or prepping for interviews. If you know you are interested in recruiting, start building your relationships at least a year in advance. All the networking tips provided in this book apply to you; use them!

Most part-time students don't seek internships due to current employment. Many schools don't allow part-time students to attend on-campus internship recruiting events, making it nearly impossible to secure a summer internship. If you have interest in a summer internship, seek out part-time students who may have had success with this in the past. A handful of part-time students typically secure summer internships every year.

Go easy on the classes

Yes, it feels like you have been in school forever, and you have reached the point where you just want to take as many classes as you can because you are so close to graduation. Do not be overly ambitious during recruiting season—you need to find balance between networking and classes. Take only one class if possible (as opposed to two, which is typically the norm). Some schools require you to be enrolled in at least one class during the fall of recruiting season so make sure to abide by the rules. If you have a demanding work schedule, take the summer before off from classes (unless you have to take classes to meet a minimum class requirement for participation) so that you can use that free time to network. It will be time well spent. As for your target graduation date, you have some flexibility in this area. As long as you graduate before or around the same time as the full-time students, you are fine. Most full-time offers are for summer/fall following graduation. In my case, graduating in December worked out well, as the firm needed new employees to start early. I was able to start in March instead of September with the full-time class. At other companies, however, starting early might not be an option.

I strongly advise part-time students to take one to two weeks off work during interview season. If you are targeting a particular industry such as banking or consulting, your interviews are likely going to be compressed into a two-week period and schedules are released a few weeks in advance so that you can plan a week off. Lucky for me, I landed with swine flu right before interview season so my absence at work was not bizarre at all. If you are not able to arrange for days off work ahead of time, you'll likely have to take a last-minute day off for interviews.

Persevere

There are numerous firms that prefer not to interview part-time students. As a part-time student, you are going to have to really prove yourself, and you are likely behind the first-year students already. You did not have a summer internship, you aren't a familiar face to firms and if you received any funding from your current firm, you will need its permission to go through recruiting (if your school even allows it). Be sure to follow the guidelines presented throughout this book to enhance your chances of success.

I landed a consulting offer with a top-tier firm, but it took a lot of perseverance on my part. From a networking perspective, I made a list of firms that I wanted to target (about 10 in my case) and identified three to five contacts at each firm through our alumni directory/ personal contacts. I scheduled two or three calls (information requests) on a weekly basis for three to four months. Your timeframe might vary slightly, depending on how many firms you choose to target. This sounds simple, but setting aside time for a phone call can take a lot of time, and given that you are also working, weaving these calls into your work day can be challenging.

My full-time counterparts had prepared for case interviews for almost a year and many already had offers. I quickly realized that I had a lot of catching up to do as none of the firms I was interested in knew who I was and I had never done a case before.

Whether case practice or technical knowledge, you must work quickly to close your gaps. If you are interested in a particular profession that recruits on campus, look for a corresponding student club. Marketing, consulting and banking come to mind immediately. Join these clubs—as they are great resources. Through the consulting club at my business school, I discovered a case coach who I hired and worked with every weekend for a few months to sharpen my case interview skills.

Get on the closed list

As a part-time student, your ultimate goal is to get on the closed list. You *must* prepare for interviews on the side, but unless you actually land an interview, you will not be able to showcase your strengths. I cannot stress enough how important networking is as a part-time student to get on the closed list. You can have a fantastic resume, but if you don't network, you are likely not going to get on the closed list. Once you get on the closed list, you are on par with full-time students and your interview performance will be judged as such. However, until then, you are not on par with the full-time class. Some full-time students, e.g., superstars, might get on a closed list with minimal networking, based on the strength of their resumes. As a part-time student, supplementing your resume with networking is mandatory if you are serious about landing a new gig.

If you don't end up on a closed list, your job search is not necessarily over (depending on the industry). Reach out to firms through your contacts to secure off-campus interviews. You might land an offer this way. Firms in many industries have hiring quotas. Not all offers are accepted, and the proportion varies each year. After recruiters get responses on their offers, they may have a few additional spots to fill. If you did not make the closed list but remained in touch with your contacts, you may have the opportunity to get an interview. If you have networked successfully, you will have a champion at the firm who is willing to fight for you and get you on the closed list or think of you when there is an open interview spot.

All in all, you are going to have to network harder than full-time students, but the payoff is worth the effort. Now go out there and get that interview!

Maneesha is a part time MBA graduate of the Chicago Booth School of Business and is currently employed at Booz & Company.

Terms

KEY TERMS & DEFINITIONS

MBA Networking Lifecycle

The period during business school in which a candidate can positively impact the Recruiter's Decision Mindset (RDM) to receive a job offer. The MBA networking lifecycle begins on the first day of a student's MBA journey and ends when the candidate accepts a full-time offer.

Half-Moon Effect

A phenomenon characterized by a single influential individual or recruiter surrounded by multiple students who form a half moon around him or her. This results in the speaker having to pivot and be relevant to a broad group of people.

Influential Individual

A person who can indirectly influence the Recruiter's Decision Mindset (RDM). Examples of influential individual include non-recruiting staff members from a firm, members of the alumni association, classmates and even professors or school staff. There are two types of influential individuals: firm-specific and school-specific. Firm-specific influential individuals are members of companies that will recruit on campus. School-specific influential individuals fall into three broad categories: students, professors and staff.

Networking

Building relationships with influential individuals to positively impact career development. It involves learning who the right people are and building personal relationships with them.

Recruiter

A person, or a member of a group of people, who is directly responsible to make decisions about who is selected for closed-list events and interviews. (Larger companies typically have recruiting teams, often comprised of recruiting managers (human resource representatives), school managers (recent alumni/junior firm staff) and/or school sponsors (senior firm staff).)

Recruiter's Decision Mindset (RDM)

A recruiter's conclusion regarding your candidacy with the firm based on a set of facts, assumptions and interactions throughout the networking lifecycle. There are four possible categories: Yes, no, maybe and Rockstar.

Relationship Hierarchy

Indicates the level of personal connection between two parties—in this case, the relationship between a candidate and a recruiter/influential individual. The relationship hierarchy is comprised of four levels: awareness, consideration, acknowledgement and support.

ACKNOWLEDGEMENTS

Special thanks to those who contributed their time, expertise and experiences to help shape this book, especially:

Corey Judson, Vishwa Kolla, Jainik Shah, Rashmi Gowda, Subu Narayana, Sujit Naik, Christine McGarry, Shilpee Magoo, Swetha Bharadvaj, Ariel Emmett, Seth Plunk, Tushar Kanungo, Monica Jain, Joshua Swartz, Maneesha Mukhi, Angela Suh, Nathan Harris, Mamta Jain, Niti Shah, Tim Darling, Jonathan Zacharias, Saundra Marcel, Elizabeth Crawford and Athena DiIullo.